IMAGINING TIME AND SPACE IN UNIVERSITIES

Curriculum Studies Worldwide

This series supports the internationalization of curriculum studies worldwide. At this historical moment, curriculum inquiry occurs within national borders. Like the founders of the International Association for the Advancement of Curriculum Studies, we do not envision a worldwide field of curriculum studies mirroring the standardization the larger phenomenon of globalization threatens. In establishing this series, our commitment is to provide support for complicated conversation within and across national and regional borders regarding the content, context, and process of education, the organizational and intellectual center of which is the curriculum.

SERIES EDITORS

Janet L. Miller, Teachers College, Columbia University (USA)
William F. Pinar, University of British Columbia (CANADA)

INTERNATIONAL EDITORIAL ADVISORY BOARD

Alicia de Alba, National Autonomous University of Mexico
Shigeru Asanuma, Tokyo Gakugei University (Japan)
Tero Autio, Tallinn University (Estonia)
Bill Green, Charles Sturt University (Australia)
Mainish Jain, Tata Institute of Social Sciences (India)
Lesley LeGrange, Stellenbosch University (South Africa)
Elizabeth Macedo, State University of Rio de Janeiro (Brazil)
José Augusto Pacheco, University of Minho (Portugal)
Zhang Hua, East China Normal University (China)

Reconsidering Canadian Curriculum Studies: Provoking Historical, Present, and Future Perspectives
Edited By Nicholas Ng-A-Fook and Jennifer Rottmann

Curriculum as Meditative Inquiry
Ashwani Kumar

Autobiography and Teacher Development in China: Subjectivity and Culture in Curriculum Reform
Edited by Zhang Hua and William F. Pinar

Imagining Time and Space in Universities: Bodies in Motion
Claudia Matus

Imagining Time and Space in Universities

Bodies in Motion

Claudia Matus

palgrave
macmillan

IMAGINING TIME AND SPACE IN UNIVERSITIES

First published 2016 by
PALGRAVE MACMILLAN

The author has asserted their right to be identified as the author of this work in accordance with the Copyright, Designs and Patents Act 1988.

Palgrave Macmillan in the UK is an imprint of Macmillan Publishers Limited, registered in England, company number 785998, of Houndmills, Basingstoke, Hampshire, RG21 6XS.

Palgrave Macmillan in the US is a division of Nature America, Inc., One New York Plaza, Suite 4500, New York, NY 10004-1562.

Palgrave Macmillan is the global academic imprint of the above companies and has companies and representatives throughout the world.

Hardback ISBN: 978–1–137–43626–9
E-PUB ISBN: 978–1–137–39927–4
E-PDF ISBN: 978–1–137–39926–7
DOI: 10.1057/9781137399267

Distribution in the UK, Europe and the rest of the world is by Palgrave Macmillan®, a division of Macmillan Publishers Limited, registered in England, company number 785998, of Houndmills, Basingstoke, Hampshire RG21 6XS.

Library of Congress Cataloging-in-Publication Data

Names: Matus, Claudia, author.
Title: Imagining time and space in universities : bodies in motion / Claudia Matus.
Description: New York, NY : Palgrave Macmillan, 2015. | Series: Curriculum studies worldwide | Includes bibliographical references and index.
Identifiers: LCCN 2015018144 | ISBN 9781137436269 (hardback)
Subjects: LCSH: Education and globalization—Social aspects. | Transnational education—Social aspects. | Space and time. | BISAC: EDUCATION / Curricula. | EDUCATION / Higher. | EDUCATION / Multicultural Education. EDUCATION / Comparative.
Classification: LCC LC191.9 .M38 2015 | DDC 306.43–dc23 LC record available at http://lccn.loc.gov/2015018144

A catalogue record for the book is available from the British Library.

To Amalia and Luciana
Your sweet souls have pushed me to question the temporal and spatial
intensities of my own journey.
I hope mine illuminates yours.

CONTENTS

ACKNOWLEDGMENTS

It is tricky to acknowledge the many people who have contributed to my journey that is the development of this book. I wouldn't possibly be able to name everyone I feel has been a part of this process. I trust that those who have been involved in this project, a life project to confuse and demystify my own world, will know who you are and will accept my profound gratitude.

However, there are a few who I must name. I have to start with Anita Sanyal, a great friend and scholar, who had the patience to read and edit my work, even while figuring out life as a new mom. Thanks so much for your time and the lovely and always funny comments on the side of the infinite pages I gave you to read. Laughing definitely is a good ingredient while writing.

I also want to acknowledge Fazal Rizvi, who sat with me during the early stages of the book and helped me sort out the important framing questions. I still remember a beautiful and profound sentence he said to me in Australia in January 2014 when I was struggling with why, and how to write this book. He said "now you have to write as there is no one watching you over your shoulders." There is so much to say about this and I am grateful for this and other wise insights that helped to propel me forward.

Of course, I must thank the editors, Janet Miller and Bill Pinar, who believed in this project from the beginning, as well as the editorial team from Palgrave. Thank you so much for the time and patience.

The writing of this book was supported by Conicyt (Chilean National Commission of Scientific and Technological Research), Proyecto Anillos en Ciencias Sociales y Humanidades (SOC 1103), Normalidad, Diferencia y Educación, www.nde.cl. The ideas expressed are the sole responsibility of the author and do not necessarily reflect those of the Commission.

ACKNOWLEDGMENTS

TIMES AND SPACES OF CONCEPTS

Imagining Time and Space in Universities: Bodies in Motion is a book that questions habitual meanings of globalization and internationalization in higher education institutions. With the abundant attention to internationalization policies and practices promoted by universities, transnational organizations, and national governments, issues such as international movement of students and faculty, internationalization of curriculum, English as a second language, the export of academic programs, among others, have emerged as significant areas of interest. However, the dominant way of addressing issues of internationalization in universities is oriented toward structural, managerial, and administrative dimensions with an emphasis on descriptive elements to facilitate more "efficient" international institutional practices. Yet limited attention has been given to cultural meanings embedded in these institutional policies and practices. This is the gap that this book intends to address. *Imagining Time and Space in Universities: Bodies in Motion* offers a critical analysis using theories of time and space to understand the implications of dominant discourses of internationalization for the construction of normative ideas of the international body, the revitalization of discourses of nation, the consolidation of notions of progress, the reinscription of traditional performances of gender, and the proliferation of imaginations of the stranger. These themes provide sites to discuss how cultural narratives are constructed and reproduced by internationalization policies and practices in higher education.

My overall argument is that time and space have been understood in separate and hierarchical modes that develop the idea of space as a key element of the showing up of the world (Massey, 2005), and time as the succession of predictable pasts, presents, and futures (Grosz, 1995, 1999, 2004, 2005; Massumi, 2002). As Elizabeth Grosz (1995) clearly indicates, "the subject's relation to space and time is not passive: space is not simply an empty receptacle, independent of its contents; rather, the ways is which space is perceived and represented depend on the kinds of objects positioned 'within' it, and more particularly, the kinds of relation the subject has to those objects" (p. 92). To imagine space as an empty receptacle containing people, objects, ideas, and beliefs affirms the idealistic and strict correspondence between bodies and geographies that demands that subjects must perform territories. On the other hand, to think and perform time as a succession, as "divisible into a static past, a given present, and a predictable future" (Grosz, 1999, p. 9) requires imagining and confining the self as being someone we already know, which in this book is read as problematic and in need of questioning. When space and time are used in their dominant conceptualizations they allow for the repetition of international practices to be fixed, and as indications of motionless cultural constructs such as nation, knowledge, and progress.

Under this dominant perspective, there is an absolute relation between time and space where time is imagined as the privileged signifier (Massey, 1994, p. 6), and space as lacking movement. On the one hand, space and its traditional ways to describe it as containing subjects, identities, objects, experiences, and practices have specific effects on the possibilities to imagine knowledge and its politics. To think of space as a "surface; continuous and given" (Massey, 2005, p. 4) brings political and social effects. My interests are oriented to understand the kinds of academic identities that are privileged under these imaginations of space in higher education institutions, the ways in which ideas of disciplines are transformed, and how the exclusionary processes become justified under these arrangements. In this book, space is questioned when it represents the idea of surfaces, as continuous surfaces, that the traveler, as the active body, walks through, find herself/himself living the "experience" of abroad, as if experience is simply located "there." This imagination of space refers to ideas that particular places have particular cultures, that particular locations are distinguishable by singularities enabling them to be differentiated one from each other. In many different ways, the prevailing ways to speak space avoid "...convening spatial multiplicity into temporal sequence; by understanding the spatial as a depthless instantaneity; by imagining 'the global' as somehow always 'up there', 'out there', certainly somewhere else" (Massey, 2005, p. 61). I am intrigued by thinking on the political consequences of thinking, practicing, living space differently.

Time, on the other hand, acts as that force hard to recognize and "see" as Derrida notes (Grosz, 1999, p. 1). I question how time acts in our representations of what knowledge, academic identities, and international movement mean; how, in whatever representation we produce, a particular notion of time is acting behind us.[1] As Grosz (1999) reminds us

> Cultural concepts of time [emphasize that time] is dynamized, [it is] seen as a virtual force and as that which builds, binds, contains, and transforms all relations, whether natural, cultural, or personal while also ensuring their dispersal, their development beyond current forms and parameters. Among them they make clear that something links the life of planets and universes to the life of organisms and their histories, and to the "life" of nonorganic or chemical beings, and this something is the endless unfolding of the new, restless transformation, upheaval, redirection and disgression, which ensures the possibility of the same even through the modes of repetition that each of these thinkers sees as central to the surprise and unpredictability of difference (Difference and repetition may prove to be two linked names that stand in for the name of time itself). (p. 5)

The political status of time and space is what is of interest here. This book raises time and space as questions, questions of the political possibilities to recreate new forms of being and producing new orientations for ways of thinking the production of knowledge and cultural politics in universities. I explore the various political and social implications of considering time as a linear succession of units, and space as a container of experiences and identities. There is much to rethink about how time and space are conceptualized in discourses of change and development when talking about higher education practices and globalization. This is a humble effort to collaborate on this discussion.

To reinvent space as contingent and relational and time as open-ended resonates with other concepts such as openness, randomness, the yet-to-come, the new (Grosz, 1995, 1999, 2005; Massumi, 2002). These theoretical arguments are visited in different themes such as, international graduate students in the United States after September 11, 2001, Chilean academics mobilizing knowledge, and women academics "returning" to their "home countries." These themes are part of the analyses produced in research studies conducted in the United States and Chile over the years. In many ways, this work is a recollection of temporalities and different locations of my research experiences in Chile and the United States. Since I have studied and worked in both countries since 1999, I have come to realize the storied nature of the politics of experiences (Massey, 1993), of movement. As a result, the constant play and questioning between limited and intelligible sets of narratives of the outsider, national, international, strange, and the like shapes this work.

UNEASY NEOLIBERALISM AND THE DISEMBODIED SUBJECT

The analyses presented in this book cannot be separated from contemporary frames of political economy. The impact of the articulation between the market's requirements and the ways universities have integrated themselves into these discourses is critical. This articulation can be easily recognized in the growing literature on globalization and higher education under titles such as "the entrepreneurial university" and "academic capitalism" (Aronowitz, 2000; Kirp, 2003; Marginson and Considine, 2000; Miyoshi, 2000; Slaughter and Leslie, 1997; Slaughter and Rhoades, 2004). Interestingly, most of this literature presents academic subjectivities as in a vacuum where the transference of neutral ideals of the corporate university may be represented and executed without interference by academics. Similarly, in universities the discursive construction of globalization and higher education as inevitably being linked to the "market's requirements" shape institutional practices in several ways, including the increasing of monitoring systems, homogenization of accountability and performance systems, standardization of curriculum processes, the increasing role of supra-national organizations in defining the purposes and processes of post-secondary education, the increasing commercialization of research and the pushing of universities to market, and so on. To operate under these ideas one has to craft and model oneself as competitive and networked.

The academics' narratives presented throughout the book are caught up in a present constituted by these discourses and practices of neoliberalism. The market presented as an "organizing principle for all types of social organization" (Sidhu, 2007, p. 205) has shifted the traditional ideas we have about academic profiles and duties. As I present different narratives of *bodies in motion*, I bring to light how institutional cultures produced through discourses of the market-oriented university have privileged the constitution of a disembodied academic subjectivity that requires that subjects narrate themselves with no reference to gendered, racialized, nationalized, sexualized dimensions understood as political expressions of their ways to position themselves in academia. By upholding entrepreneurial assumptions to create the profile of the professor is a way to separate the body from what professors do. I am troubled by the ways a business orientation shapes the imagination of the academic by identifying the market-based assumptions inherent in academic profiles. A professor today is seen as,

[...] being energetically confident and single-minded but giving the appearance of being consultative and democratic. It means taking on the role of a cultural diplomat, talking about 'special relations' and 'partnerships' while carefully sorting and weaving the right mix of cultural differences to give the appearance of openness to all cultures and classes, men and women. (Sidhu, 2006, p. 305)

Certainly, these new ways to define academic profiles makes a difference in terms of how we understand what we do in academia and have important consequences on the ways universities justify evaluation and monitoring systems. Interestingly, in 1993 in the Chilean context Brunner et al. (1993) were already reconfiguring the definition of the social expert with specific references to academic practices:

The social expert can be a traditional academic, but frequently he is not. Now he is usually a researcher who acts as a consultant, an advisor, as a source of information or as a broker within a major network of specialists. His office is an open and multidimensional space since he operates in many different places: he attends meetings at the ministries, attend the parliament as an expert, he is hired by a consultant office, he has a network of clients, he travels national and internationally, attend seminars of specialists, and writes in different media sources. Briefly, his life is not limited to the production of knowledge. His surroundings demand to promulgate and promote those knowledges, to apply them where it is possible and, in any case, to make them available to potential users. (p. 10, *my translation*)

The ideas presented in this paragraph refer to a person who crafts himself as an entrepreneur. This business orientation to explain academic practices in the field of Sociology in Chile is strongly affected by contemporary notions of universities as connected to market requirements. As these ideas have expanded and wielded more authority, particular images of academics have gained a privileged position in research universities. This has had critical institutional consequences.

As a result of the appealing character of the discourses of successful academic subjectivities, the traditional division we/they (Humanities and hard Sciences) is being transformed. In this transformation, the Humanities and Social Sciences have been pushed to occupy the language of efficiency and competitiveness particularly in the areas of academic publishing, grant applications, innovation, and knowledge transfer. The traditional division I am referring to is what Donna Haraway (1988) explains as,

the imagined 'they' constitute a kind of invisible conspiracy of masculinist scientists and philosophers replete with grants and laboratories. The imagined 'we' are the embodied others, who are not allowed *not* to have a body, a finite point of view, and so an inevitably and disqualifying and polluting bias in any discussion of consequence outside our own little circles, where a 'mass'-subscription journal might reach a few thousand readers composed mostly of science haters. (p. 575)

This oppositional way of talking about the Humanities and hard Sciences, well known as it is, has taken different intensities and variations from its traditional version. Through my research I have come to see that while other ways to comprehend this division operate, they are not as distinguishable as one may think.

Along with changes in the meanings of being an academic under the assumptions that neoliberal forces operate in universities, higher education institutions have twisted their missions to adjust themselves to the new *times* for universities. For instance, under this frame curriculum has tended to follow a standardized format where notions of knowledge have changed in particular and critical ways. Such forms of reasoning knowledge—through the idea of curriculum as only a matter of organization, development, and standardization—signals a particular way to reframe issues related to what knowledge is, how it configures ideas about who the student is, and who produces knowledge.[2] In this scenario, universities are prompted to redesign curricula and degree programs that would be to "serve corporate hiring needs, [...] that condone corporate influence over curriculum and program development by accepting corporate-funding programs, fellowships, and faculty lines, [...] that adopt profit-oriented corporate values, [...] that instill corporate culture in their students and staff" (Nelson and Watt's, 1999, p. 90). Decisions about curriculum design, therefore, are easily recognized as guided by corporate values. For these corporate dispositions of higher institutions operate, they require that different forms of domination such as, gender, race, nationality, sexuality remain invisible. This serves as a way to secure neutrality. As feminist scholars have argued, to maintain these neutral ways to define oneself and what we do is the way corporate practices benefit themselves (Duggan, 2003). In other words, success in the implementation of these corporate values depends on the invisibilization of relations of power.

As universities use the language of the corporation and make it their own, the idea of the unmarked and disembodied figure appears as a relevant concept to maintain a rhetorical separation between managerial agendas and cultural politics in higher education institutions. By presenting administrative and management matters as technical rather than political or cultural, neoliberalism's orientations emphasize efficiency and personal (individual) responsibility as desirable. And, by doing this, the dynamics of class, race, gender, nation, and sexual politics in which these neoliberalism's practices are embedded are made invisible.[3] The ways in which universities are managed today are presented as primarily a matter of neutral, technical expertise, that require to be framed as "separate from *politics* and *culture,* and not properly subject to specifically political accountability or cultural critique" (Duggan, 2003, p. xiv). Academics' narratives presented in this book enable the exploration of new intensities and variations of already naturalized processes of corporatization in academia through the separation between politics of knowledge production and cultural politics. Academic narratives provide us with a possibility to understand micro political and cultural meanings of the university. These analyses offer tools for both paying attention to embodying practices and analyzing the workings of higher educational institutions in the related contexts of globalization and neoliberalism.

A MOVING HISTORY

This book takes up the question of how internationalization processes have come to shape discourses of the successful university today. It offers a critical perspective of the construction of dominant understandings of internationalization practices and how they connect to specific rationalities such as, neoliberalism (Duggan, 2003). Particularly, I explore on the relation between the production of specific academic identities, the understandings of knowledge, and those forces that produce and constrain them. It is my argument that new orders imposed by the neoliberal project instill specific discourses and practices in universities. The market acting as an organizing principle for higher education institutions without a doubt changes logics and ways to understand what we do and who we are. What troubles me most is that because of this, universities are being transformed in profound ways and in many manners removed from political and cultural debates. In other words, the ways in which the university is orienting itself today affect the meanings of what professors do. Universities supporting modernist projects (based on principles of autonomy and rationality), uncritically directs our attention to the production of a specific type of knowledge, a specific idea of inquiry, and as a consequence a specific kind of academic identity. In this way, internationalization practices have become a particular institutional practice to develop certain dimensions of the university and to make others (such as the economic ones) to flourish. As the market and its operations compel specific research agendas and contents for the courses, universities are being transformed both on its missions and management structures.

The recognition of the international context as a decisive factor in the unfolding of the processes of subjects' production and the circulation of power is vital. Most important, in today's interconnected global world, time and space have become important analytical tools to understand how power circulates at the intersection of a range of social differences and institutions. In different ways time and space direct questions as to what the political possibilities for institutional subjects today are and how institutions are entangled with the market's requirements. As the common way to describe international changes is characterized by transnational corporations and global competition, massive innovations in computer technology and communications, international terrorism, and the notion that subjects are mobile, make us raise political questions about movement within universities.[4] The ways to imagine the global context and how these ideas shape the attitudes of governments and policymakers who decide appropriate domestic policies for education, immigration, employment, and the like is critically important for those who have to perform and live these definitions in universities. In a world of increasing interdependence and competition, international discourses and practices can only become more important particularly in the case of universities where current processes tend to focus on internationalization as one of the major forces responding to the paradigm of globalization.

As the processes of globalization and intensified international competitiveness have led to widespread mobility, universities as critical institutions in the reproduction of market mantras (knowledge society, innovation, productivity, among others), requires the troubling of particular cultural practices related to movement. For instance, globalization, or what Saskia Sassen-Koob (cited in Clifford, 1997) has called as the "internationalization of production" (p. 7), has spurred qualified immigration into the United States producing new forms of racial conflict and intensifying questions around the legitimacy of those entering the country. At the least attending to the dynamics of living time and space in different ways because the movement pushes us to questions for the ways certain subjectivities become a problem in this context.[5] The multiplicity of identities and subjectivities embedded within the frame of internationalization forces one to rethink how faculty and students might be the subjects and agents of these processes.

What this book does is shows examples on the ways discourses of internationalization of higher education markets have come to alter ideas of knowledge, faculty, and students (Sidhu, 2006) through particular narratives. It also questions how dominant notions of space and time that inform the present configurations of internationalization processes in higher education institutions, serve to reproduce uncritical discourses of nation, progress, and subjectivity. In many ways this book argues that time and space, as lived experiences, are always political conceptualizations. I seek to interrupt the naturalization of internationalization discourses in higher education institutions in relation to spatialities and temporalities.

THE INTERNATIONALIZATION MOVEMENT

Universities—through research, increasingly international and mobile academic professors, global research networks —contribute to the development of this global scenario (Altbach, 2002). Because of the great emphasis placed on international cooperation, universities and educational organizations have focused on internationalization as part of their policies to place themselves within the context of globalization.

Today, internationalization has become a primary goal of academia because different motivations originated after events such as global terrorism, new commercial agreements between countries, the expansion of frontiers in terms of production of goods, and so on. And, no less important is the fact that international education has become a commodified product to be sold by itself. This is expressed in the intensification of movement between nations where the "natural" path is that few countries dominate the current technological, educational scenario, and those are mostly Western industrialized nations. As expected, English language has become the medium of instruction and research. This reinforces the binaries and conditions of power created around developing countries, perpetuating their dependency on developed ones. This discourse of "convergence" has produced that few developing countries have been able to analyze how internationalization discourses and practices may affect, facilitate, and ultimately benefit their own processes of expansion, development, and implementation of new possibilities within the global context (Rizvi et al., 2001).[6]

In a very idealistic dimension, factors supporting the considerable expansion of the international rhetoric in universities are closely linked to the interest in integrating the notion of "global interdependence" in the curriculum and a "philosophical commitment to cultural perspectives in the advancement and dissemination of knowledge" (Iuspa, 2014, p. 14). As institutions of higher education in the United States have realized that international interdependence is a political dimension of the internationalization processes, issues of awareness of living in a global community, the political scenario of living in an interdependent world, and the recognition of how this determines the lives and decisions of people who are immersed in it, has a direct impact on the ways university define its policies. As mainstream discourses on internationalization issues announce "the gravest issues we face are essentially all international issues requiring global cooperation, centrally-focuses initiatives, and a worldwide commitment" (Rahman and Kopp, 1992, p. 1).

As most of the data indicate that the facts supporting the need to internationalize education are more commercially oriented, it is important to look at how different institutions have configured the spread of the imagination of people moving around the world. For instance, Open Doors[7] in 2002 reported that more than a half million international students will spend more than $11 billion on tuition and living expenses in the United States. This report presented that more than two-thirds of foreign students receive most of the funding for their education from personal and family resources. While it is true that there are a variety of educational products being offered in the international educational market, the recruitment of international students historically represents a major industry. This has been a stable pattern over time for the United States.

Most interesting is a report published by IDP Australia[8] back in 2003, which forecast that the global demand for international higher education will increase from 1.8 million students in 2000 to over 7.2 million by 2025. Today the Open Doors Report (2013–2014) states that over 886.052 international students are welcomed in the United States Much of this growth comes from China, India, South Korea, Saudi Arabia, and Canada; with the United States continuing to be one of the major beneficiaries. These projections are highly significant for they reveal a changing landscape of higher education in which commercial concerns become ever more dominant. For instance, Phillip Altbach (2001) has stated that

> It is not surprising that those motivated by commerce, in government and in the private sector, would concern themselves with ensuring that "knowledge products" are freely traded in the international marketplace. If these interest groups have their way, higher education in all of its manifestations will be subject to free trade discipline just like bananas or airlines. The rules of the World Trade Organization (WTO), and its related General Agreement on Trade of Services (GATS), it must be remember, are legally binding. There is a danger that regulations relating to higher education will be included in an international agreement "under the radar" and without much analysis. When something becomes part of the WTO regime requirements and regulations, it is subject to complex arrangements. The implications for higher education are immense, not only because of a new set of international regulations but because the university will be defined in an entirely different way: the overriding goal of GATS and the WTO is to guarantee market access to educational products and institutions of all kinds. (p. 3)

Within this framework some universities may well see "international business as a means of ensuring financial survival when facing problems of declining revenues from domestic students, governmental pressures to maximize student population and the uncertainty of research funds" (Davies, 1992, p. 182). Income available to the university from a wide range of international sources, such as "overseas student fees, student related grants, project grants, consultancy overseas, continuing education programs overseas, research projects, technology transfer-licensing to overseas companies, franchising courses to colleges in other countries, agency arrangements" (Davies, 1992, p.182), have become a very important component of university financial systems. With all these elements in mind, international education has become a very critical aspect of university's agency, particularly within the globalization framework, transforming the very nature of universities. The fact that the flow of students overseas move largely from the developing countries to the industrialized nations is a topic that need further discussion.[9]

FLEXIBLE DEFINITIONS

As expected, internationalization of higher education has become a very heterogeneous and contested practice. The most basic and consistent element in the use of international education is to "refer to multiple activities, programs and services for which the primary focus is international" (Arum and van de Water, 1992, p. 201). However, Altbach (2002) proposes that a more conceptual and critical understanding of globalization and internationalization is needed to make sense of the varied and complex ways in which they affect higher education in the United States and worldwide, and of the various ways universities are responding to these pressures.

Unsurprisingly, the literature contains a number of definitions of what is most generally called the *internationalization of higher education*. A working definition that has been generally accepted by practitioners as well as researchers in this field is one that focuses on the transformation process: internationalization is "the process of integrating an international/intercultural dimension in the teaching, research, and service of the institution" (Knight and de Wit, 1995, p. 15). Within this framework it is possible to distinguish at least four dimensions constituting the international education: (a) studying abroad; (b) language education; (c) international students; and (d) internationalization of the curriculum. Examples of internationalization include policies relating to recruitment of foreign students, collaboration with academic institutions or systems in other countries, and the establishment of branch campuses abroad. Other definitions have come to problematize some ethical, political, social, and cultural assumptions related to the definition of internationalization of higher education. For instance, Ann Francis (1993) proposes that these processes of internationalization should prepare the community for successful participation in an increasingly interdependent world. Others offer an understanding of these processes as requiring integrating interdisciplinarity in the teaching and research mission of universities (Patrick, 1997), curriculum plurality (Sadiki, 2001), and the like.

As expected, academic programs within colleges and universities that are aimed at providing an international perspective and cross-cultural skills to students are becoming increasingly popular (Arum and Van de Water, 1992). Yet, some authors argue that the goals of international education are still at the level of rhetoric (Altbach, 2002). Criticisms by certain scholars posit that "international education has a somewhat unusual position in higher education. While recognized as an important sphere of activity, international education tends to be handled by administrative offices at the top of departments of languages and international affairs" (Arum and Van de Water, 1992, p. 201). I would add that this leads to lack of efforts to develop a critical international practice among students, both domestic and international.

What is important for the purpose of this book is the commitment expressed by universities to internationalize. This commitment provides the broad landscape in which my concerns are located. Universities have developed "mission statements that often point to the presence of international students and scholars as evidence of their current level of internationalization" (Klasek et.al., 1992, p. 10). However, the institutional mission statements remain general, and rarely refer with any specificity to the need for special spaces of professional development, and a critical discussion on the disadvantages in terms of professional experiences for this population (Kuhlman, 1992; Sidhu, 2006, 2007; Sidhu and D'Alba 2012). More importantly, the question should be oriented toward cultural processes embedded in institutions as a result of this academic movement.

Without a doubt, the events on September 11, 2001 in the United States, turned a spotlight on international education, and raised the question of how foreign student enrollments in US institutions were impacted. Several stricter controls on international students have been implemented since then. The expanded regime of regulation affecting the lives of international students in the United States is worth noting. Fear for personal safety, in particular, was a common issue in international students' experiences. As William Cummins (2001) concludes in his article "Current Changes of International Education,"

> Because international education in the U.S has essentially languished over the last decade, American colleges and universities are not well-prepared to help their students understand the events associated with September 11. New regulations may make it more difficult for Middle Eastern, as well as other international students, to study in the US. It has been said that the more salient impact on the future flow of students to US is likely to be the extent to which the U.S

markets its educational opportunities and the overall state of the world economy which influences the affordability of pursuing studies in the U.S. (p. 3)

Notably, this statement not only reproduces the current ideology of international education in terms of its economic implications, but also stresses other features of universities such as cultural, social, class, and national repercussions associated with these specific problems, particularly with respect to how these new regulations pose a threat for international students. I would argue that the September 11, 2001 events intensified the attention on international students, but this did not necessarily mean that this group now had more constraints than in the past. It was simply that such constraints were overlooked in preceding times.

THE TIMES AND SPACES OF UNIVERSITIES

The conversation presented in this book then is about the important effects of universities as international institutions on the configurations of knowledge,[10] subjectivities, academic lives, and their relations in those institutions. The relevance given to corporate and instrumental discourses in defining the purposes and commitments of higher education institutions requires a critical look at the effects of these transformations. As universities become a strategic component within a corporate global discourse, neutral languages create academic and institutional cultures where the privilege of masculine, disembodied, and technical discourses come to play. These emphases shape experiences and ways to narrate who the subjects are and what they do. And, as a consequence, they produce a particular way to orient academic lives, purposes, and institutional achievements.

My central argument is that the use of theories of time and space to complicate conversations about internationalization practices in universities offers a possibility to unearth the assumptions operating behind recognizable identities, institutional dispositions, and affective practices that support internationalization as the way universities explain their own processes of advancement.

In many ways, we conceive time and space as acting behind our backs. This allows us to perceive, produce, create possibilities, and limits to ourselves and others. This is important because as we move through different understandings of time and space we also orient ourselves in a different direction that may guide us to other constructions of ourselves, to switch the purposes of our actions, and to finally produce a new politics of the production of knowledge and institutional subjectivities. I think it is relevant to explore not only on how specific notions of time and space inscribe bodies and practices in universities, but more importantly, how these bodies and practices are imagined as possibilities and through which internationalization practices as we know them, are possible. We need to renew concepts of time and space if we want to develop alternative ways of understanding the inscriptive and developing discourses that currently dominate the higher education field.

To explore on the workings of dominant discourses of time and space in this book, I employ methodological approaches that include discourse analysis[11] and ethnographic interviews to examine how they maintain orders and normalcies that elevate certain practices about who we are and who we may become while devaluing others, and the implications of these processes in the context of people moving across geographies. Because discourses of internationalization of universities within a globalized culture dominates the horizons of institutional policies and practices, describing how time and space is given meaning and experienced by *bodies in motion* living in such particular discursive scenarios is absolutely central to a cultural consideration of universities today. I situate my analysis in institutional documents and interviews with people whose academic work has been affected by movement. The coming chapters include the critical questioning of assumptions embedded in institutional documents, interviews with international students from Colombia, Kenya, Japan, and Turkey in the United States after September 11, 2001, interviews with female and male Chilean academics in Chile belonging to different disciplines, and women academics from Social Sciences and Humanities from different universities in Chile. My intention in presenting their stories has to do with that they destabilize and contest a uniform way to think of time and space. I am not saying that they actually live space and time differently, but because of their experience of movement it seems to me that we can question the political implications of living under the restrictions of specific institutional regulations.

What I explore in the pages that follow are stories of women and men who have constructed different trajectory paths within universities, whether, as graduate international students, junior, or senior faculty. I use their narratives to question normative understandings of time and space and how they have specific effects on the ways we produce ideas of movement, progress, and knowledge, among others. In other words, I am attentive to the ways in which the establishment of universalizing ways of imagining time, space, and its relations underpin narratives, stories, and possibilities.

It is important to make clear that academic identities or institutional processes are not the object of research here; rather, they are excuses for me to enter the questioning of the ways these identities and practices are possible as a result of the ways we think and put to work notions of times and spaces.

Throughout the book, I allude to spatial and temporal experiences of people and how they disentangle the relations between space and identity, and time and progress. Subjects, especially those subjects who are thought as mobile, are spatially and temporally contingent. This means that they are in the midst of becoming, that they do not signal themselves as in reference to one point in time and space. This has political consequences for the ways we imagine knowledge, politics, and subjectivities.

CHAPTER MAPPINGS

This book is a reminder that we should not neglect to critically question concepts that we rely so heavily on to sustain our realities. To think time and space otherwise implies to question those exigencies, the forces generated by the ways we think space and time. Time and space act as conditions that produce possibilities and limit ways to think about our lives, to think the ways bodies are enculturated, and how certain practices gain an unquestioned prevalence.

To accomplish my purposes I have considered different stories told by people that I named as *bodies in motion*. They represent different academic statuses and institutional locations. The participants have produced their narratives in different geographies and times. This is a compilation of my work since 2000 till now. To be able to name these pieces of information as belonging to different times and spaces has enabled me to question my own assumptions of time and space when producing research questions, when performing research, and when defining myself and others as *bodies in motion*. To be able to apprehend this previous research information and reuse it, questioning critically the frames of its production, is part of the incredible journey I have come to finish with the writing of this book.

In chapter 1, I start with a description of those theoretical and methodological tools on which I rely. I introduce several theories of time and, along with other work of feminist geographers, queer, and gender theorists. These theoretical tools are essential to shape the understanding of the following chapters. Narrative interviews are used to look for assumptions about different topics of interest and the relations across them (Fairclough, 2003, p. 40) as well as assumptions that make them unique. The analyses proposed are directed to construct complexity and avoid the production of tidy linear narratives. I intend to contest power relations and disassociate hierarchical constructions of international bodies and movements. In this sense, my analysis of the interviews is "intertextual, in that [it seeks] to identify mediation, or the movement of meaning" (Fairclough, 2003, p. 30) as it is recontextualized across the interview texts.

In chapter 2, I explore how the construction of "the international" dimension in U.S universities is related to particular temporal and spatial imaginations. Policies and practices that seek to develop an international dimension in universities are traditionally imagined as the congregation of different nationalities, which are not separate from popular prefigured imaginations of countries represented as fighting, poor, sick, and/or exotic nations (among other descriptions). These practices of institutional internationalization—viewed as containing attractive, authentic, and contradictory cultures, lives, and essences—perpetuate the construction of the "international" based on discrete nations, national trajectories, and essentialized bodies. These imaginaries not only perpetuate the idea of the "world at a glance" (Casey, 1999, p. 80), but also reproduce "natural" relations between people and nation. The significance of this chapter is that it questions taken-for-granted notions of time and space as separate from each other and as divisible that allow the persistence of institutionalized essentializations of nations and people under the rhetoric of internationalization.

Chapter 3 discusses the processes international students undergo when deciding to go to the United States to complete their graduate degrees. I do not follow the conventional approach to address particular processes international students follow when deciding to study abroad. This means that beyond the explanation of the process itself I want the reader to capture those elements that provide a sense on how different discourses and regulations create specific experiences to be lived by international students from the very beginning of their journey. I use interviews from four international students from Kenya, Turkey, Colombia, and Japan.

In chapter 4, I present a discussion on the notion of international students as constructed by research studies in the United States I suggest that different discursive practices, new migration policies, and media have constituted an image of the international student that has been intensified by the threat posed by global terrorism. I argue that the production of the category of international student needs to be problematized to avoid the perpetuation of a strange, static, and inert subjectivity. In this chapter, I turn my attention toward critiquing research about international students that I argue mainly involves a remedial approach where they are constructed as problematic subjects because of their condition of being outsiders. I believe that even though research discourses differ in some important ways from policy discourses, the notion of the international student is still insufficient to represent them more critically in terms of the contemporary fragmented realities experienced by them.

In chapter 5, I trouble the "path" that defines who international students and faculty are in relation to places. I explore how the taken-for-granted understandings of place, as a container ready to be filled in, act on us to normalize and anticipate positions for ourselves and others. In other words, I explore how the imaginations of place define what international students and faculty might become when "going abroad" or "coming back." It is my contention that the category of international students and faculties obtaining their degrees in countries different than their own are intrinsically related to ideas of place. For instance, much of their narratives signal spatial codes to refer to their experiences, "arriving," "returning," "home country," "host country," "origin," "departure," and so on, all of them indicating starting and ending positions. Discourses emanating from institutional policies and research studies that describe international students' experiences frequently speak to a naturalization of particular experiences within implicit spatial frames of reference, such as nation, race, social class, sexuality, and the like. In this chapter, this is critical since spatial imaginaries demand constant construction and reproduction of the taken-for-granted meanings of place, which in turn revitalizes other essentialisms.

Chapter 6 complicates the absoluteness of time when related to histories of movement of women academics. Those travels initiated by women to obtain their graduate degrees abroad and their subsequent experiences when they are "back" may serve to reflect more in the *becomings* (Grosz, 1999) than in a static perpetuation of what it means to bring knowledge "back" to the nation. My argument is that the dominant constructions of the university as a *"place"* that remains untouchable by the experiences of movement of academics are related to traditional understandings of time as "divisible into a static past, a given present, and a predictable future" (Grosz, 1999, p. 9). These representations and uses of time, not only perpetuate repetition and circularity of discourses of progress, nation, and instrumental knowledge in academia, but also deprive us of "becoming something other, we know not yet what" (Rajchman, 1999, p. 48).

In chapter 7, I present a discussion on the forces that come to play when talking about the production of knowledge in universities understood as international identities, particularly through the act of writing. I use women's interviews to explore on the meanings of academic writing today. My argument is that contemporary ways to reason universities as international institutions have important effects on the configuration of knowledge, subjectivities, and their relations. Discourses of internationalization of higher education that use institutional arrangements to promote specific practices in order to call themselves successfully international, such as international networks and circuits to publish academic work, designing and implementation of international collaborative research, high-level indexed publications, and so on, produce the idea that these are the "natural" institutional outcomes and aspirations for professors. Such institutional practices create the conditions for a new institutional developmentalism (Sidhu, 2007) where the reconfiguration of international practices has taken on the work of managerial tools. Institutional cultures produced through these discourses have privileged the constitution of a disembodied academic subjectivity that requires subjects to narrate themselves with no reference to gendered, racialized, nationalized, and sexualized intensities. I explore on how this dis/embodiment is narrated and problematized by women through their acts of academic writing, particularly in disciplines related to Humanities and Social Sciences.

In the concluding chapter, I explore the implications of transnational spaces and times and their implications on the ways we conceptualize and represent various subjectivities and practices of internationalization in higher education. In making sense of the dimensions of time and space, I seek to move forward from a separation of both to explore new ways of thinking that requires the broadening of academic imagination to create new representations of practices in universities. I contend that the regulation of subjectivities and practices in universities through single trajectories created as effects of using dominant conceptualizations of time and space leaves no opening for an active politics. For instance, by "characterizing space as 'abstract geometry' and place as 'sites of shared experience' conveniently ignores the ways in which differences of gender, age, class, 'race' and other forms of social differentiation shape people's lives" (Weems, 2010, pp. 559, citing Bondi and Davidson). Uses of traditional understandings of time repeat and circulate normative ideas and practices in academia. To trouble normative ways of using time in universities requires the uses of time as a force, which means that time can be thought of as something else (Deleuze and Guattari, 1987; Grosz, 1999), not only as locked in the idea of the succession of specific units. Therefore, one of the goals of this book is to question the "promise of the new" (Grosz, 1999). As Elizabeth Grosz (1999) proposes, "to rethink temporality in terms of the surprise of the new, the inherent capacity for time to link, in extraordinarily complex ways, the past and present to a future that is uncontained by them and has the capacity to rewrite and transform them" (p. 7). By theorizing about space and time and their integral relation I speak of multiplicity and openness as new configurations that may set off new social processes.

CHAPTER 1

METHODOLOGICAL TWISTS AND THEORETICAL TOOLS

This chapter outlines the theoretical and methodological tools that serve as a foundation for this book. In order to understand the claims and counterclaims contained in the different chapters of this book, I present here a necessary theoretical synopsis for the readers. *Imagining Time and Space in Universities: Bodies in Motion* presents critical theorizations of time and space, which question the access we have to different experiences of international movement. These theorizations reveal the inherently unstable nature of dominant discourses regarding trajectories and traveling. I argue that internationalization discourses produce certain institutional subjectivities and practices due to their implicit ideas about time and space embedded on their dominant definitions. These dimensions have been understood in separate and hierarchical modes, which mean that producing accounts of meaningful experiences with institutional progress necessitates the advancement of an understanding that sees space as a key element of the showing up of the world[1] (Massey, 2005) and time as the succession of predictable pasts, presents, and futures (Grosz, 1999). For instance, the common idea that tells us that academics or graduate international students who move from one place to another *carry* specific attributes and characteristics of their geography with them makes us hold on to the idea that there is a strict correspondence between place and identity (e.g., Peruvians act as Peruvians because they come from Peru). Moreover, the notion that "advanced societies" are apparently ahead in terms of chronological time makes us imagine that those who come from "second world countries" are behind, that they in some way belong to the past. These ideas lead universities to design specific politics and policies for international students and faculty based on essentialized notions about the cultural and social attributes of the subject. The passivity with which the subject is thought in relation to the production of spaces and times requires a critical look. As many authors have indicated, the subject's relation to space and time cannot be inert (Grosz, 1995; Massey, 1994, 2005; McDowell, 1999). Such conceptualizations would suggest that we approach spaces as empty receptacles and time as the fragmentation of life. Imagining and feeling space as an empty signifier means that we occupy different locales thinking that we are independent of them and that location and site have nothing to do with the ways we perceive space. However, as Elizabeth Grosz (1995) notes, "the ways is which space is perceived and represented depend on the kinds of objects positioned 'within' it, and more particularly, the kinds of relation the subject has to those objects" (p. 92.). To think of space as a passive container of experiences, identities, and practices neutralizes the operations of power as it produces specific subjectivities and confirms the mapping of particular geographies in terms of their relationships to other spaces. To think of space in this way prompts us to imagine space as a homogeneous force that bears no effect on internal productions and external connections. This way of imagining space has critical effects on the ways we conceptualize identity and its political uses (Massey, 2005). If space is "something we reach" it means that we occupy that space by acquiring specific and given social and cultural positions. Continuity of movement, as a political device, is left out of the picture in these visions of space. The positions that people occupy then are just things that happen. Identities thus become a referent independent of reality, of its production.

On the other hand, to think and perform time as a succession, as "divisible into a static past, a given present, and a predictable future" (Grosz, 1999, p. 9) requires imagining and confining the self as predetermined subject (Davis, 2000; De Landa, 1999; Grosz,1999). This book actively challenges and problematizes limited and static notions of time. I question such paradigms because they imply that the recognition of specific cultural attributes and dispositions of the subject are intelligible. To fragment life and to tell a story of movement means that we need to present subjects as belonging to particular spaces (that contain specific identities) and to imagine them as units in progression. Reinventing time as an open-ended dimension resonates with other concepts such as openness, randomness, the yet-to-become, the new. To experience the world as moving, transitioning, means that the world "is temporally contingent" (Sharma, 2014, p. 149). Thus, the meanings we give to the experiences we live are similarly tentative. Elizabeth Grosz (1999), when discussing approaches to time as concepts of difference, explains that "...each in his way [referring to Deleuze, Bergson, and Nietzsche] affirms time as open-ended and fundamentally active force—a materializing if not material—force whose movements and operations have an inherent element of surprise, unpredictability, or newness" (p. 4). The question arises then that if uses of time resonate more with the indeterminacy of the future, in what ways are the past and present in dialogue with those practices and subjectivities produced because of internationalization discourses?

When space and time are used in their dominant conceptualizations they allow for the perpetuation of international practices as fixed elements, and as indications of motionless cultural constructs such as nation, cultures, knowledge, and progress. Universities then become "orientation devices which take the shape of 'what' resides within them" (Ahmed, 2006, p. 132). The ways we tell the experience of institutional space and time are showing us the available discourses we have to reposition ourselves. In such fashion we can ask, how are bodies transiting different spaces and times aware of the movement that is left out to position them? What are the political effects of lacking movement? If time and space are seen in a relational and nonlinear manner, in what ways do these notions affect our production of research questions? If subjects coincide with their own variations, as Massumi (2002) suggests, then how do we produce knowledge about those subjects? If we focus on the unfolding of the subject, what are the underlying ideas of time and space that we should consider?

These questions and theoretical arguments are foregrounded among different themes in this book such as in the experiences of time and space of graduate international students in the United States after September 11, 2001, in Chilean academics' mobilizing knowledge after completing their graduate degrees abroad, in women academics "returning" to their "home countries," and in the analysis of different institutional documents related to regulations of international bodies, and institutional documents on internationalization. As a result, I complicate the constant play between restricted sets of narratives of the international, the strange, and the national.

One of the main strategies to produce meanings and to have access to the conceptual ordering of experiences in these studies was the interview. Interviews were presented to the interviewees as a possibility to tell and expand stories of their lives with openness and detail. Thus, I give a special location to the idea of the production of meaning through the act of interviewing. I did not intend interviews as "mediating meaning but as means of creating knowledge in a discursive field" (Tsolidis, 2008, p. 273). As I use interviews performed with different people from different territories, points of departure and arrival, I was interested in assumptions about movement, actual places, promising futures, and nostalgic pasts. I looked for different concepts of time and space and the relations across them (Fairclough, 2003, p. 40) as well as assumptions that made them unique. For instance, the number of spatial and temporal metaphors that internationalization discourses use to describe processes and practices becomes a frame to analyze the workings of power (Gee, 1999). Flows, networks, webs, links, streams, and flux all reveal how time and space are presented as a way to apprehend the cultural experience of millions of people who are in the process of movement.

As my interest is directed to those narratives from people who have gone through different kinds of academic journeys, in this book I come back to interviews at different points in time (2002, 2003, 2006, 2010, and 2011) and in different locations (US and Chile). Such an approach allowed me to revisit my own assumptions about space and time to "make real" the conversations we had over those years. I have now shifted my focus of analysis to question and analyze my own way of asking questions and the assumptions embedded in them to provoke ways of narrating experiences of time and spaces for those participants. In many different ways, I am now looking at how power was structured under assumptions of my own thinking of time and space.[2]

All the participants I interviewed share some characteristics that are important for these analyses: they are produced as *bodies in motion*. This means that I consider movement as vital to the production of meaning about what constitutes their narratives. It is an exercise in moving away from the idea that bodies inhabit spaces in static ways and that they always describe their experiences under a normalizing temporal order. By using the expression "bodies occupying spaces" (and this would be a dominant way to understand space), I refer to those ways of narrating these experiences as "arriving" and "departing." These conceptualizations indicate that what defines "the body is not the movement itself, only its beginnings and end points. Movement is entirely subordinated to the positions it connects. These are predefined (Massumi, 2002, p. 3). This has specific effects on the ways we comprehend our own experiences of movement. To "depart" means to leave and be separated in many ways from a territory, from pasts, from communities. To "arrive" means that we enter a different territory that gives us a different name, where we become strangers and owners of stories of "foreignness." In so many ways, *bodies in motion* are forced to coincide with cultural labels (the immigrant, the stranger, the foreigner) with critical consequences on the cultural and social constructions these bodies have about themselves. On the contrary, as Massumi (2002) suggests, "when a body is in motion, it does not coincide with itself. It coincides with its own transition: its own variation" (p. 4). Thus, the stories I present in the book are stories about the politics of time and space. To coincide with those given institutional categories for international people is a way to maintain the strict imagination of the common experience of time and space. In the case of those experiences of people I interviewed spaces that we normally think of as stable are put into question. Ideas of home, the university, the hospital, and the classroom are presented as highly politicized spaces of movement.

To experience space and time as static, meaning that space is something produced ahead of our arrival and that time has definite points in our telling of experience, creates specific possibilities and conditions to create institutional lives. Bodies leaping from one place to another, being attached to geographies to construct themselves, gendered bodies producing spatial politics, bodies experiencing the political affection of major world crisis,[3] are issues arising from the conversations with the participants. These are the stories that I use to learn about the political possibilities we have depending on the conceptualizations of time and space that operate in our backs.

Thus, the analyses proposed in these studies are directed to construct complexity and avoid the production of tidy linear narratives. As these narratives are produced and caught up in a chain of movement, the production of meaning intends to follow similar paths of rhythms and pulses. As I move through the texts produced in conversation with different temporalities and tempos, I intend to contest power relations and related hierarchical constructions of international bodies and movements (Browne et al., 2010). In this sense, my analysis of the interviews is intertextual, in that it seeks to identify mediation, or the "movement of meaning" (Fairclough, 2003, p. 30) as it is recontextualized across the interview texts.

STUCK IN A MOMENT

In many different ways and levels this work is a recollection of temporalities and different locations of my research experiences in Chile and the United States. Since I have studied and worked in both countries since 1999, I have come to realize the storied nature of the politics of movement as an experiential phenomenon (Massey, 1993; Manning, 2009). Thinking about my own experience as an international student, I began with questions concerning the way people in academia thought about who I was and enacted various different definitions of who I was supposed to be. Even though there are several major research studies written about international students and the politics of international universities, less has been written about the ways those multiple cultural and social sites in which this community is positioned are articulated in specific regimes of space and time. Describing how international students' difficulties affect their academic performance, how language is an important element in their "adaptation," and the many cultural crises to which international students are exposed seemed increasingly less compelling to me, for I realized these studies failed to capture the complexity of the improvization and agency bodies enact under these circumstances. By the time I started to formulate my research questions I had been in my graduate program for three years and the problems of international students, how they were perceived and in what ways they were reconstructing themselves, became more important to me. The substance of personal conversations with graduate international students provided me with a foundation for a critical study of the international students' lives in an academic environment and in a country that was not their own.

When I came back to Chile as a professor, I started to deal with institutional politics and I realized that producing knowledge was, in many different ways and dimensions, problematic. I started to rebuild my research questions following my own spatial and temporal tracking of the institutional experience. I realized I could not "tell an experience" by using the discourses available to me. In other words, I realized the power of gendered, raced, and classed stories when telling the narrative of international movement. I thus noted that the experience of what constitutes the world in terms of "going abroad" and "coming back" was space and time contingent and thus more and more political. I became more conscious of the uses of terms related to time and space to describe what I was living as an academic returning to her "home country." To be simply read as a body from a starting and an end point did not help to clarify the constant state of flux I was under nor did this reading address the ways I was contesting my own way of producing knowledge, and the complex understandings of the travel itself. To come back to a "definite" point, to perform whatever I had learnt, did not seem to me a sufficiently complex narrative to tell. I then decided to push these understandings to explore how dominant notions of time and space may affect the kind of possibilities I had to narrate myself. I decided to explore what other academics who have moved themselves to different territories have to tell. I was particularly interested in searching for differences among genders, disciplines, number of years within academia, and particular characteristics of institutions. My guess was that there must be something I could learn by posing the question on how different universities (private and public) may provide different perceptions of time and space. This particular set of interviews that I used for this book are oriented to ask men and women from the fields of medicine, nursery, sociology, psychology, education, arts, theater, aesthetics, economy, physics, social work, literature, engineering, and anthropology from two different universities in Chile about the meanings attached to travel, the limits of the discipline in relation to the present pressures of the international way to produce universities based on new policies on institutional accreditation and publications standards. How did international trajectories help them to question their sense of themselves and how did they produce new ways of politicizing what they do within their disciplines? One important feature in their responses was how academic writing became an important political site to access critical ways of questioning institutional practices. I also used university policies and research studies to tell more about the ways institutional spaces and times are created for those people who do academic travel. These texts set up cultural conditions that go beyond regulation and monitoring. Policies and research, in this case, act as cultural producers of subjectivities and communities. This series of texts, documents, and interviews provided the ground for me to explore the meanings of the experience of movement, and the limits that dominant notions of time and space impose on our lives.

INTERVIEWS AND PEOPLE

Using interviews allowed me to understand how the experiences of *bodies in motion* were shaped by different discursive practices that constrain and expand in multiple ways and degrees their daily lives of the participants in my study. The interviews were useful in documenting the complexities and redefinitions of their lives. Interviews, in this case, can be seen as spaces where knowledge production was always under the gaze of power relations and regimes of truths. Interviews were shaped by the conceptualizations of times and spaces we had operating in our backs. The ways to refer to the relation we have to space, the temporal manners we frame our experiences and trajectories are possibilities to critically deconstruct the notions of time and space. As I moved through these interviews and texts I came to understand the ways gender, sexuality, and race were very useful to explain the relations to space and time. In so many ways, these conceptual tools organized people's own notions of the meanings of the past, present, and future. Thus, I do not intend to apprehend a true self or a true experience, rather I set out to engage within the framework of these participants' imagination of time and space and explore in what ways they may offer other ways to live institutions. In other words, by looking back at the interviews I prepared several years ago I was able to see how my way of asking was "informed by a background conceptualization of space and time" (Massey, 2005, p. 154). As a critical consequence, chances for the participants to answer and become something different were almost impossible. The words I was using to allow the possible selves for them to be expressed was something I took as political and critical for my analyses.

For example, the kinds of questions I posed to the participants who were graduate international students at the time the interview took place were based on specific notions or references to spatial nouns and verbs that defined the questions and specified the answers. In the case of those interviews with international students in the United States and the original protocols I prepared for the interviews, I presented four main topics organized as follows: (a) their stories in their countries; (b) the processes involved in coming to the US; (c) who they were in relation to the places they inhabit; and (d) their experiences relating to mobility and study in a foreign country. As the participants' particularities emerged, the interview questions became specific to their stories. In other words, the initial questions themselves became too static that could not reflect the unfolding of their experiences. Then, I shifted to questions that reflected more of their particular experiences as international students in their departments within the college of education in a US institution. For instance, with Sarah (a graduate international student from Japan) we discussed how the fact of considering herself *westernized* in Japan affected her experience in the United States. I found this point particularly important, so I asked questions about *westernization* in different ways to the rest of the participants in the remaining part of the interviews. Although my interviews were based on certain basic questions, our interviews frequently took unexpected or unanticipated turns. For example, we would sometimes talk about our lives, our research, how we were coping with certain situations or issues encountered by other international students in academia. As I anticipated, there was much relevant information that often emerged in our informal conversations after the record button was turned off. Most of the times, the interviews began with spontaneous interactions between the participants and myself. Although the structure of the interviews was still based on my established research questions, these evolved through the negotiations that characterize conversations between friends.

Later in my research process, I interviewed men and women in Chile so the questions became consciously related to the ways different disciplines and different higher education institutions (administratively speaking) give political and cultural contours to tell their experiences of movement. Some of the questions that oriented our conversations were designed to understand how knowledge production, either through methodology itself or through the creation of research questions, had been modified because of traveling. Other questions were intended to understand the ways institutional gender arrangements affected the meaning of being an academic today. The power of certain questions I asked was of significant importance. For instance, when I asked the participants to talk about the meanings of writing to think about themselves as academics was particularly interesting. I just opened the interview with this question and follow-up questions were almost unnecessary. Something happened in the ways they were affected by this question. It articulated how participants actually live institutional space and time and the ideal spaces and times the act of writing brings with it. These passages are visited in chapter seven.

All the participants not only answered questions that I prepared, but also formulated through dialogue their own conceptions of their experiences and raised new questions I had not considered. This process highlighted the relational nature of knowledge created through the interaction of people in the conversation where different notions of time and space are negotiated. The revisiting of these interviews made me question epistemologically the process of interviewing transforming in some ways my understanding of the process itself. Now I conceive it as a practice in which we (researcher and participants) are critically reproducing dominant notions of time and space that create meaning in specific ways. This understanding also helped me rethink the notion of the subject as someone we know. Now that

I could see my own process of asking questions in different times and geographies, I came to question the basic assumptions and ideas of what an interview is, which is often regarded as a unilateral process of asking and answering. It was not enough to me to problematize how dominant notions of time and space were participating in the production of meaning. That is why I came to the notion of narrative as a possibility for me to question senses of times and spaces when producing meaning.

NARRATIVES

As a possibility to explore the complex nature of interviews and to produce meanings and problematize the times and spaces of the stories we tell, I used the notion of narrative to expand the ways I understood the production of knowledge through interviews.[4] I think that the notion of narrative allows us to think of interviews in a different way, as Stewart (1996) tells us: "Narrative, [...], is not just the recounting of events but the thread of a thought that traces the precise turn of event in which the possible becomes probable, the mythic reveals itself within the ordinary, and the immanent or emergent is instantiated in the actual" (p. 12). In this sense, to think of interviews as a way of a narrative expands the production of meaning available to the researcher. It is not that the interview texts are complete or that they portray a clear example of whatever the interviewee wants to say. Rather, that was the very moment where other possibilities to expand meaning emerged. As I came back to the interviews developed in previous years I was able to capture how meaning was travelling through the texts. Thus, interviews took a different form. They were not separate units to be analyzed. As a thread I was able to understand the abstracted signs that embodied the ways we speak time and space and how they give life to a collective shape of the institutional world of universities. As Katheleen Stewart (1996) notes, "Rather than complete or 'exemplify' a thought, narratives produce a further searching" (p. 32). As I went back to these interviews I had the chance to question the ways we take positions when we interview research participants, and how we assemble specific orders to talk and tell trajectories of life. As I move along the texts I became troubled by how my own imposition of tempos and spatialities in the questions was presented to the interviewees. As such, possibilities for the new meanings remained invisible.

In this sense, stories told by the participants were productive to the effect that I was able to trouble my own way of asking stories that represented linearity, order, sequence, and hierarchy. As I was able to see my own impossibility to ask questions using other assumptions about time and space to produce something different, I was able to move somewhere else, that is, the notion of narrative became a way to give a political outcome to the interview text. As Katheleen Stewart proposes (1996)

> ...narrative is first and foremost a mediating form through which "meaning" must pass. Stories, in other words, are productive. They catch up cultural conventions, relations of authority, and fundamental spatiotemporal orientations in the dense sociality of words and images in use and produce a constant mediation of the "real" in a proliferation of signs. (p. 30)

In so many ways, to question the frames to produce interviews through normative notions of time and space is a manner to work beyond representational concerns and to open up possibilities of "knowing" social and institutional lives. As Stewart (1996) notes, "Picture how the authority to narrate comes of having been somehow marked by events, in mind if not in body, and how the listeners, too, place, themselves in the scene of story and follow along in its track so that they too can be somehow marked with its impression"(p. 32).

To use the tool of narrative as a way to go back to the interview texts and refresh my own way of "searching for meaning" allowed me to relocate my initial research questions and renew my political interests. I was able to go back to that space I had built with these interviews in terms of meaning and question how I was constructing or reconstructing specific ways of unifying memory of territories and correspondences between subjectivities and places (Keith and Pile, 1993). As I went back "in time" to the interviews as narratives I was able to question my own ways of ordering subjects, territories, stories in particular notions of space and time (Bakhtin, 1981). This "looking back" has particular possibilities to produce an understanding of meanings that were woven inbetween the texts, as an intertextual structure of meaning (Kristeva, 1980). These insights were not visible to me until I used space and time as analytical tools to assemble the traces and trajectories of my own ways of questioning and producing stories.

In this second moment of revisiting previous interviews I came to understand that "The story does not express a practice. It does not limit itself to telling about a movement. It *makes* it. One understands it, then, if one enters into this movement itself..." (Stewart, 1996, p. 210 citing de Certeau 1984, p. 81). To understand interviews as narratives allowed me to pay attention to how questions were always referring to a moment in time and to a way of relating to space. What does it mean to be a graduate international student in the United States? What can you say about "coming back" to your home country? All these questions are based on a trace, on a way to build a story, a way to go back and forth between meanings and constant productions of who you are in relation to your own telling of the experience. In other words, I was able to see the political dimensions of constantly narrativizing the world we live in, how life becomes available, and what are the uses and purposes of it.

SOMETHING ELSE

As I moved through my own academic trajectory I came to understand the impossibilities of my own ways of framing and giving contours to my research questions and how "problems" were possible to be expressed, seen, and researched. Space and time, at some point became central. Space was first. I came to see that the ways I was experiencing territories and places were profoundly connected to the limits and possibilities of producing myself and the social and cultural world around me. This process also became political. First, came the realization that space and place were categories to question the cultural production of institutional subjectivities. Later, came the possibility of time as a category to understand how I structure and give life to stories of past and future as the possibilities to frame my institutional present. Time and space allowed me to rethink and reinvent questions I had about myself as a researcher in relation to structures of institutions and ways of telling and describing experiences.

Space and time, as I moved along, allowed me to ask very specific questions. The kinds of words one uses to express intentions, purposes, and problems in Social Sciences research had specific references to notions of space and time. All of the sudden notions of belonging, detachment, progress, even my role as a researcher were an effect of specific notions of space and time. Dominant notions of space and time, then, produce particular traces to frame objects of study, research questions, ideas about the researched and the researcher, about contexts, and the like. In so many ways dominant notions of space and time act behind our backs pushing the meanings of what we see, forcing the meanings of those conceptual relations we create, preventing ourselves to move in a different direction, compass, and rhythm. For instance, the constant reference to territories with a defined cultural mark is a way of insisting on the idea of correspondence between bodies and lands. This is part of the usual way to refer to oneself as a subject on the move. But also this way of describing oneself has to do with how questions are being framed to produce that kind of answer. The subject as the product of the question (Colebrook, 1996) takes us to think of the importance of our own ways of framing the world. If we use different notions of space and time, space as relational and time as becoming, then what are the type of questions we produce and as a consequence what kind of subjects become possible? These questions are certainly important whenever we are documenting experiences of those people who travel around the world because of academia. There must be something we are missing whenever we foreclose on the experience of movement because of the use of dominant notions of time and space.

Space in its dominant version refers to vacuum, emptiness, surface, no entity and lack thereof (Massey 1994, 2005; McDowell, 1999; St. Pierre, 1997; Tsolidis, 2008). Likewise, time brings to mind ideas of sequential linearity, of particular units arranged in a line of progression (Grosz, 1994, 1995, 2004, 2005; Manning, 2009; Massumi, 2002; Sharma, 2014). These are the ways we have been told to organize space and time. When we travel to a different territory, we can swear we are crossing lines and entering a different space. When we tell the story of movement we are convinced that we have moved to a different moment in life. If we do not critically address how places have been imagined and how times organize ways of narrating stories, our understanding of a subject's capacity to creatively improvise will be minimal. We should definitely ask ourselves how we are producing research when the intersection of time and space are of relevance. In what ways then do our research questions maintain the rigid articulation between subjects and certain places, to certain times and its articulations?

Bodies in Motion intends to rescue the notion that interviews are "spatial practices" (Clifford, 1988), and as such need to be understood as "time practices" as well. Both, time and space provide a position for the speaker to organize their experiences to be narrated and for the researcher to make sense of it. In other words, the interviewee and the researcher perform specific spaces and times. They get attached to the specificities of how their bodies have been told to narrate themselves. My work thus seeks to trace the invention of bodies in motion, through narratives of outsiders in order to question the totality of an "experience" told by individuals moving internationally.[5] As a consequence, I am interested in the possibility of exploring those assumptions of time and space that operate behind our backs when telling stories and narratives. The partiality of time, and the sense of lack of space have political consequences for the ways we frame our possibilities to do research, to name problems, to continue establishing casual relations, and to maintain meanings and ideas attached to identities. In this case, the operations of power are sustained through specific notions of space and time. They provide specific rationalities that Foucault defines as "ways of thinking about and acting upon one another and ourselves" (Barry et al., 1996, p. 5). The important point in here is that the opportunities subjects have to think about who they are in relation to spaces and pasts, presents, and futures are political in such a way that institutions become spaces for containing identities; for example, the foreigner has to occupy a given experience that is charged with particular ideas of race, class, gender, sexuality, and the like. Time, institutional time, is also loaded with specific ideas of progress and advancement for the international scholars and students. This way to rationalize the experience of people on the move has important consequences for the ways we think of research and how it transforms what we do in universities.

How can we mark the space of an identity, of a problem we need to study? How can we stop time, to cut time to search for answers to our questions? How are space and time relational in that both construct the final idea of what we feel and interpret out of the world? The authority of dominant conceptualizations of space and time can be mapped. This is the intellectual exercise I have proposed to myself.

By describing several examples of multiple, entangled temporalities and spatialities—graduate international students and women writing in different disciplines in academia, among other topics—*Bodies in Motion* questions the dominant notions of time and space that prevail behind the narrations of people connected to academia in different ways. This is an exercise that demonstrates the complex ways people experience time and space.[6] In so many ways, this book explores how the political aspects of our narratives shape our lives. As Jameson (1981) states (cited in Stewart, 1996),

> In the fundamental mediation of events, identities, and social orders in narrative form, the question is not how narrative rearranges preexisting subjects and objects but how things are written into the "ideology of form"; how the aesthetic act draws the density and texture of sociality, history, and cultural politics into itself and carries their weight as an immanent subtext—a "political unconscious." (p. 181)

WHAT I DO

In chapters three and four I will go back to a qualitative exploration of the experiences of international students in a graduate school in the United States. In this research, I looked at how the conceptualizations of time and space of a group of graduate international students from different countries (Turkey, Japan, Colombia, and Kenya) are shaped and transformed by studying overseas particularly after September 11, 2001 in the United States. I was not only interested in learning about the ways the international students narrated their political trajectories when coming to the United States, or the ways they feel their lives and professional experiences are understood, valued and/or marginalized in the United States, but also on how moving into a different country may have connected to other possibilities of understanding of who they were in relation of space and time. I was particularly interested in those specific tensions between discourses about international students and international students' stories told about themselves. In other words, how did particular notions of space and time operate as a way to regulate and discursively position subjects in motion.

In chapter two, I analyzed documents from different sources and institutions. For instance, I read the ways universities talk about international people and presented some of the policies and regulations about their academic studies after September 11, 2001. I also examined policies that reward universities for their successful internationalization efforts and explore the ways authorities are pushing specific ideas about people coming from other countries. In addition, I analyzed research studies that define international students' identities and critically expose those problems related to the experience of international movement.

In chapters five, six, and seven, I presented another portion of my research dealing with Chilean academics mobilizing knowledge after completing their graduate degrees abroad. I was particularly interested in women academics "returning" to their "home countries." I wanted to know how academics in Chile have been thought of different places and times through ideas of the corporate university. Particularly, I explored how the performing of institutional time and space represented a way to subject women to specific ways of producing academia. I used excerpts from interviews with women academics in Chile from two different universities to show how the uses of time and space sustain, and probably revitalize, neutral and universal discourses of progress, the nation, and instrumental knowledge. The chosen interviews are part of a larger project whose purpose was to understand the uses of policies and practices of internationalization of higher education in Chile.

DRIFTING TO MEANING

As this book traces meaning produced over the years, meaning has been produced below ground. Meaning has been woven across the years, territories, disciplines, and bodies. As Derrida (cited in Hodder, 2000) has shown, "meaning does not reside in a text but in the writing and reading of it" (p. 704). Then, writing became a process in and of itself.[7] The very process of writing gave me a specific space where I connected and created tensions between texts and theory. I believe that the time I spent writing served to illustrate the importance of the process of writing itself. The time I was engaged, in silence with my own words and text, provided a space in which to make conscious articulations, to question, and to challenge my own thinking. If data from interviews were full of the participant's understandings of themselves, of interactions, as well as their interpretations, of the materiality of everyday life, then writing was the process through which I re-created and destabilized what had been taken-for-granted regarding their stories. As I was troubling my own ways of framing questions using notions of time and space, a constant production of something was happening.

To a certain extent, I became aware that my writing had been determined by the idea of space as experience and time as the fragmentation of life. In writing I have seen myself balancing these two imaginations. This was a tension created in the process of writing that involved multiple dimensions of what it means to be a researcher including the social and historical conditions within which the different topics of this book are immersed. To play with narratives and theoretical constructions has been an enormous task, because it has involved a constant look at what was, what has become, and what is currently important to me. The state of an *outsider* has also been relevant to the process of writing. *Belonging* to a language, nation or culture, and the ways in which cross-cultural experiences forge notions of self are all important considerations in the process of writing. This idea of living in dialectical tension between cultures, languages, and places has brought a political consciousness when writing about *bodies in motion*.

To conclude, a discussion of further implications and critical reflections that have emerged from the process of thinking about space and time as relevant to question ways to become institutional subjects is central to the theoretical imperatives of this book. I have come to look at the process of understanding/interpreting as a way of being. I see that knowledge has emerged from the engagement between the participants, texts, and myself. Meaning itself is therefore an interactive process because it emerges out of interactions. In this case, meaning/knowledge as a consequence of human activity is never demonstrable but always problematic and dynamic. Thus, truth becomes a matter of consensus on beliefs and values that responsible people would reach in a given situation. In this way, I stand in relation to the participants, and texts, and how I conceive and define their responsibility for representing value judgments about them has caused me to rethink my own role as a researcher. To work under these commitments creates the idea that knowledge belongs to those who are in the context and the researcher is the one who helps to translate what they are experiencing as knowledge.

The relevance of having gone through the process of this analysis is that the object of study is understood as something enacted, something that unfolds continuously. For this reason, my understanding of *bodies in motion* is that they are inherently ambiguous and their stories only coincide with their own ambiguity. This makes writing a complex task. What are the words I need to use to represent this ambiguity and variation, that transition? From this perspective, to do research is to problematize context and the aspects of people's lives that has been taken for granted.

CHAPTER 2

THE USES OF NOSTALGIA: RE-ENACTING SPACE AND TIME

This chapter explores how the construction of "the international dimension" in universities is related to particular nostalgic temporal and spatial imaginations. As I already noted in chapter one, the most common institutional international initiatives are developed, mainly, through the exchange of students and faculty, the internationalization of curriculum, and the export of programs of study (e.g., English as a Second Language). One concern with these policies and practices that seek to develop an international dimension in research universities is that they uncritically imagine "international" space as the congregation of different nationalities, which are not separate from popular prefigured imaginations of countries that suffer from war violence, poverty, disease, and/or posses an "exotic culture," among other characterizations. These practices of institutional internationalization—viewed as containing attractive, authentic, and contradictory cultures, lives, and essences—reproduce and naturalize a way to imagine and organize global space that reinscribes and reenacts particular ideas of nation, border, region, and more. These imaginaries not only perpetuate the idea of the "world at a glance" (Casey, 1999, p. 80), but also reproduce "natural" relations between people and nation. This way to imagine "international" space uses a form of nostalgia that reproduces a desire to reenact a "real" place (nation/country/culture) in an absolute time. This form of nostalgia produced by institutional discourses stresses the notion of homeland and home as "the maternal return, [the return to] the matrix of wholeness" (Valis, 2000, p. 120). By stressing this absolute place in time, the "permanent condition of loss and exile" is exacerbated (Valis, 2000, p. 120). This form of nostalgia is in charge of reproducing the firmly established imaginary picture of the world. Such a nostalgia assumes "that space and society [were] mapped on to each other and that together they were, in some sense 'from the beginning,' divided-up" (Massey, 2005, p. 65). Nostalgia is represented as "a return to an original point of departure or home [as] belonging, [as a way to live] in our primitive world, the timelessness or eternal return of [the] mythic being" (Game, 2001, p. 230). In this sense, what is reproduced is the idea of memory of home as a "structure of feeling, which retains its character of cultural mourning" (Valis, 2000, p. 130). Most importantly, this idea of memory incites and feeds unproblematized narratives of correspondence between bodies and territories.[1]

To reproduce the imaginings of global space composed by bounded places with "their own internally generated authenticities" (Massey, 2005, p. 64), and to insist on its repetition through discourses of institutional internationalization is to hold onto and "mourn the loss of the old spatial coherences" (Massey, 2005, p. 65). Thus, I argue that nostalgia, as a specific institutional cultural practice (Stewart, 1988), reproduces essentialisms whose reproductive dimensions lie in the belief that space and time exist independent of people's ways to imagine them. Nostalgic narratives are grounded in the assumption that stability of territory and identity is real. Thus, recirculating languages of nation as an indissolubly contained unit that suggests illusionary correspondence between territories and identities has become the dominant language of movement in universities.

Then, the purpose of this chapter is to trouble the uses of nostalgia as an institutional practice that stresses the memory of home through the repetition of naturalized spatiotemporal configurations of the "international" space in universities. This practice not only "retains its character of cultural mourning, but also strengthens [...] the desire to return" (Valis, 2000, p. 130); it also offers the promise of homogeneous places and cohesive populations around specific attributes and dispositions of people. I explore how specific ideas of time and space influence our senses to frame imaginaries of the "international" in university settings through this notion of nostalgia. The conclusions of this analysis direct attention to the following questions: Why is it that when thinking about other countries from "an international perspective," these nations look as if they exist in a different time? When thinking about people from another country, why are they imagined as authentic and in strict and inherent coherence to a place?

I use two sets of data. First, I use pieces of institutional documents from the American Council of Education and the Association of International Educators, NAFSA, that detail both the problematic assumptions that underlie the category of the international body, and the representations of international space in universities. Second, I use interview excerpts from graduate international students from Turkey and Kenya who were in the United States completing their degrees to show how dominant notions of space and time work on our backs to narrate experiences of movement. As these notions of nostalgia act as a secularized mourning for spatial and temporal coherences (Valis, 2000) on peoples' imagination, its uses have critical implications for the ways unproblematized narratives of movement, nation, and identities are re-inscribed in institutional policies. I connect these two sets of data to complicate how public and institutionalized discourses organize and affect our daily private life narratives.

ORDINARY PICTURES OF NATIONS

Universities today, as active "players" within the global economy, promote internationalization policies as a desirable standard to meet. In this environment, higher education institutions actively promote the movement of students and academics (among other activities), which is perceived as a highly desirable signifier of institutional success. It is common to find institutional reports that document aggressive policies to attract and stimulate study-abroad programs and international exchanges. However, institutional discourses and policies usually ignore the "geopolitics of intellectual practices and their effect on other geographies, other people, and other cultures" (Sidhu, 2007, p. 61).

Focusing on those internationalization practices whose purpose is to gather people from different nations in an institutional international space, most discourses are oriented to emphasize the benefits of socializing with the *stranger*. There is an implicit belief in the idea of "contact" as a value to pursue under the frame of internationalization. For instance, it is very common to read statements in university mission statements such as, "Students learn about international events, cultures, and issues through the various extracurricular activities offered on and off campus and through their contact with international students" (Measuring Internationalization at Research Universities, 2005, p. 15). Another common statements is, "... [international practices are meant to] provid[e] opportunities for US and international students to learn from one another outside the classroom" (p. 15).

A number of clichés can be found under the umbrella of internationalization efforts in higher education institutions. The following are but a few examples:

"Contact with individuals whose background differs from my own should be encouraged;" "Students can understand their own culture more fully if they have studied another;" "Study abroad programs are the best way for students to encounter another culture;" "International education can explain the root causes of basic global problems such as overpopulation, poverty, climate change, and disease;" "Courses with international content usually focus on a specific region of the world;" "International learning helps prepare students to become responsible global citizens;" "International learning makes students appreciate more of other cultures;" "Learning other cultures helps students tolerate ambiguity when communicating with a foreign person."

The assumptions embedded in these institutional discourses construct universities as providers of international contacts and transnational flows, which reinforce the idea of an unproblematized "out there." In this way, discourses on internationalization rehearse the two dominant discourses where space and place are separate. Under these, place expresses the concrete, known, bounded and real, and space is perceived as the abstract, the outside of a place (Massey,

2005). Moreover, time is a way of passing and as the succession of standardized units from which it is possible to narrate pasts, presents, and futures construct narratives of progress and development (Grosz, 1995, 1999; Lowenthal, 1985). These abstract imaginaries activate historic continuities by creating an ancient past and a promising future. These imaginaries, as one may think, are not naïve. They provide material possibilities to produce subjects who perform specific identities, identities that are mostly essentialized and naturalized, lived as prescriptions.

One of the documents I analyze, "Securing America's Future: Global Education for a Global Age," from the National Association of International Educators (NAFSA) (2003) presents recommendations to promote study-abroad programs. As expected, these initiatives take into consideration the events of September 11, 2001 and signal, " [...] it has become more and more clear that our country [the US] simply cannot afford to remain ignorant of the rest of the world." The document follows, "The generation that will lead our country tomorrow [...] must receive an international education today. They must have opportunities to learn about other countries, other cultures, and other points of view from direct experience as an integral part of their higher education." The underlying assumption of "authenticity" that international students provide to the local student is critically relevant because those policies regulating international students act as the limits to be lived in.

In a different sentence, the document makes its politics explicit:

> By virtue of our power, the United States is truly the world's leader, but we cannot lead a world that we don't understand for very long. If we are to have any hope of living in safety and security, any hope of exercising our world leadership in the constructive manner in which we all aspire, then we will have to take steps to understand the rest of the world much better than we now do.

The exceptional status of the United States as the nation that leads the rest of the world, posits the figure of other nations in specific hierarchical positions, and as such, locates the "less developed" subjects from other nations as securing the global dominance of the United States.

Moreover, later in the opening of the NAFSA Annual Meeting in 2003 Marlene Johnson, Executive Director and CEO of NAFSA adds, "...American's lack of knowledge of the world represents a national liability in the war on terrorism." The tone of the international discourses after the events of September 11, 2001 in the United States affirms an interesting connection between securing the future of the nation and the need to know the "out there." Even though this idea in itself is very problematic, it is necessary to highlight how international initiatives in universities are thought as a response to a crisis in national security.

The idea of getting to know the world implies the explicit reproduction of a modern universalistic idea of the world that is a *coherent* place, as a space divided in explicit easy-to-recognize units with predictable cultures and pre-given identities. Getting to know this world takes on a nostalgic tone in that there is a mourning for territorial coherence. Nostalgia acts as a "...social emollient and reinforces [national] identity when confidence is weakened or threatened" (Sarup, 1996, p. 97). As Katheleen Stewart (1988) notes, "In a world of loss and unreality, nostalgia rises to importance as 'the phantasmal, parodic rehabilitation of all lost frames of reference'" (citing Foster, 1985, p. 228).

I turn now to a different document from NAFSA (2007), "Internationalizing the Campus: Profiles of Success at Colleges and Universities," which profiles those campuses that received the Senator Paul Simon award for successful campus internationalization practices. The document addresses four US institutions and documents their strategies and accomplishments. In the following, I present iconic sentences from two of the awarded institutions to illustrate the uses of nostalgia through dominant imaginings of space and time.

One of them is Sunset College (USA) that, among several other activities, documents the experiences of a group of students going to Kenya to work in a rural area of the country. The faculty member in charge of the program explained that "the trip was a 'deep cultural dive' for his class" (p. 10), and that one of his students replied, "It was dusty and dirty and fantastic" (p. 10). To exoticize places and people is one of the effects of the dominant framing of time and space related to experiences of movement. To think nations as containing cultures, rituals, practices, and identities is to continue reproducing and idea of the world that exists without intervention. Such a way of thinking constructs *those* people and places as strangers, as the unknown. While it would seem untenable to presume cultural uniformity and narrow understandings of other places, this line of thinking assumes specific conceptualizations of time and space.

A different paragraph explains, "International students are becoming more aware of their own culture. Korean students go back home over Christmas break, visit grandma in the village and ask 'Can you teach us a folk dance?'" (p. 10). One assistant professor of history stated "I've had a number of students who are really eager to go out and save the world (p. 11). Another professor commented, "Many taboos are being broken... We see the Chinese now differently from 50 years ago, not as very poor but as mathematicians. We see the Indians or Russians as chemists or software engineers. As we get to know more about them, we associate better attributes to foreigners" (p. 13). It is key to remember that these are award-winning campuses from well-regarded universities, exemplar for others yet they also need to be constituted as providing evidence of how "the international" is exoticed and essentialized in official documents.

In a different example provided by this document, the University of Oklahoma's president narrates his experience when meeting an international student from Malaysia. He asked the student "how many American students have you gotten to know really well while you have been here?, to which the student replied, "Not very many. We international students tend to be together. Boren [the President] recalls the young men expressed regret that he had not gotten to visit an American farm nor seen any real cowboys" (p. 44). From then on, among the institutional activities organized to welcome international students "We tell everybody to dress up like cowboys and cowgirls. The international students really look like the part" (p. 44). Besides the uncomfortable idea of the exotic Other this institution is presenting I want to focus on the look at the discriminatory practice proposed under the valuable dimension of international practices for universities.

The document then goes on to describe the university's accomplishments: "At every major academic convocation, a phalanx of international students bearing their countries' flags marches behind bagpipers and the Kiowa Blacklegging Society, a group of Native Indians in feathered headdresses" (p. 46). Of course, the immediate response to these provocative passages is to refer to the very obvious ethnocentric, colonialist, and capitalist assumptions that reproduce the *other* as always in need of being saved, helped, cured, guided, and so on; the caricaturization of naturalized identities; the claim of authentic social problems others have (poverty, sickness, etc.), and the like. However, in this case, I want to focus my attention on the nostalgic impulse behind these stories. Nostalgia, as a modern orientation revitalizes the idea of an absolute past and a contained space. In other words, nostalgia for the cowboy, for the folk dance, for the "real" Chinese student, acts as an impulse to preserve essentialized ideas about imagined past coherences between the self and places, and in doing so, it acts as a way to retain a sense of identity.

ANXIOUS NOSTALGIA

Nostalgia, as a cultural practice, orients us to something that "once possessed detail, a specific shape, time and place" (Valis, 2000, p. 130). This is a hegemonic way to exacerbate the idea of home as a preexisting entity. Deleuze and Guattari (1987) remind us, "home does not preexist: it was necessary to draw a circle around that uncertain and fragile center, to organize a limited space" (p. 311).

This form of nostalgia as an essentially modern register requires certain elements to express itself (Tester, cited in Radstone, 2007): "a linear sense of time, a sense of the present's deficiency, and the presence of artifacts from the past" (Chase and Shaw, cited in Radstone, 2007). In this case, the stories told about internationalization by higher education institutions present ideas of an invented past where congruencies and coherences between people and nations function as a way to align trajectories of colonial power. It is "an imagination which, having once been used to legitimate the territorialization of society/space, now is deployed in the legitimation of a response to their undoing" (Massey, 2005, p. 65). The idea of the present's deficiency is implied in the notion of national insecurity and vulnerability presented in the documents that address issues of internationalization; thus, international is formulated as a space to be conquered. In other words, nostalgia comes to "... reaffirm identities bruised by recent turmoil when 'fundamental taken-for-granted convictions about man, woman, habits, manners, laws, society and God [are] challenged, disrupted and shaken'" (Lowenthal, 1985, p. 13). The idea of the stranger, as someone who has to be known, is a way to portray the international body as "undecidable" (Sarup, 1996, p. 10), as someone who is "physically close while remaining culturally remote" (Sarup, 1996, p. 10). In many ways nostalgia reestablishes a sense of truth about selves, spaces, and times.

Thus, the linkages between imaginations of the nation and identities sustained by nostalgia are historical and cultural forms of positioning. For instance, institutional nostalgia, as a particular form of cultural claims for home, intersects inevitably with other manifestations such as colonial, gendered, classed, and nationalized differences. As Ahmed (2000) explains, "If we think of home as an outer skin, then we can also consider how migration involves not only spatial dislocation, but also temporal dislocation: 'the past' becomes associated with a home that is impossible to inhabit, and be inhabited by in the present" (p. 91).

The idea of nostalgia inscribed in modern notions of space and time relates to other conceptions such as progress and development. For instance, notions of progress usually "employ some idea of temporal sequence and a principle of evaluation where change from worse to better can be determined" (Johnson, 2001, p. 93). This formulation of an evolutionary characteristic of places is sustained by universal ideas of space and time. As Sarup (1996) reminds us, "The past is the foundation of individual and collective identity, objects from the past are the source of significance as cultural symbols" (p. 97). The preservation of imagined coherences from the past through essentializing discourses is a way to retain "real" spaces with "real" people in "real" time; it is a way to preserve selves who create and enunciate space. This not only perpetuates repetition and circularity of spatial orientations such as nation and time as progress, but it also requires imagining and confining the self as someone we already know (Grosz, 1999), which is problematic. These dominant conceptualizations of space and time invigorate modernist attempts to universalize the imagination of the relations between people and spaces. What I draw from the ways institutions portray the international space is that they require a way to present universities as containing specific and recognizable identities coming from discrete regions of the world. In Massey's (2005) words it relates to the idea that "First the entities exist, in their full identities, and then they come into interaction" (p. 72). From this point of view, cultures and nations are "imagined as discretely different, separated one from each other and internally coherent" (Massey, 2005, p. 64).

The international dimension of universities as places for spatial play (Hetherington, 2001) invents a space, which congregates essences and cultures. As Hetherington (2001) explains, "In these forms of spatial play, we witness a modernising utopic put into practice in which future-oriented ideas about order, improvement and development [are] expressed through certain kinds of planned social space and the discourse surrounding them" (p. 51). The international space in universities represents the aspiration to create a better society through the idea of putting everybody together. It is a way to fabricate the "ideal space" here and now. This represents "how society might be improved in the future" (Hetherington, 2001, p. 51).

The international place in universities represents people as if they are coming from the past and welcomed to the future. The international space in higher education institutions imagines places that have stopped evolving or have been moving at a different pace. The "international place" goes back in time and reenacts a space. As Doreen Massey (2005) states, "...but places change; they go on without you...A nostalgia which denies that is certainly in need of re-working" (p. 124). Imagining regions and countries as backwards is "...to deprive others of their ongoing independent stories" (Massey, 2005, p. 125).

The way the international space in universities is organized and ordered refuses to acknowledge vital characteristics of spaces, namely their dynamism and multiplicity. All nations and cultures as spaces have come to be through endless interconnections. The presumption of the autonomy of spaces has enabled nostalgic accounts of places as autonomous entities, as points of departure, as origins and isolation, locales that are in need of critical attention. There must be other ways to secure or guarantee an eternal future than through static accounts of coherences between people and nation.

AWAY

In this section, I use interview excerpts from two international students while they were completing their degrees in the United States. I use these stories both to complicate those discourses announced in policies presented in the section "Ordinary Pictures of Nations" and to show how the participants themselves police the strict relation between territory and identity. I use narratives from a female graduate student from Turkey and one male graduate student from Kenya. In many ways, these are stories that tell us what is at stake when people recognize themselves as corresponding to a territory, and what it is that we have to secure when responding to the logic of belonging to *a place in time*. Thus, I engage in an exploration of the meanings of being *away* and of those practices attached to the discourses of home, identity, and the nation.

A TURKISH WOMAN NARRATIVE OF SPACE

One of the dominant narratives that my respondents used to express being *away* was articulated through the concept of homesickness. References to music, dance, and food are predominant artifacts from which they built a strict relation between territory and identity, as the Turkish participant in my study recalled:

> Some types of music I didn't listen to in Turkey, but here I listen to this music, [and it sounds] nice and authentic, you know? It's because I miss it, and also it's because I see the authentic value of it when I'm here [in the U.S.]. Do you know what I mean? Like, in Turkey I wouldn't listen to folk music, or I mean Turkish folk music, or you know Oriental music....I am not sure [the reason why I do this] because if I do not listen to Turkish folk music when I go back, then does that mean that my view has changed?, or am I doing these things that I didn't do [in Turkey] because I am homesick. I don't know.

To bring sacred objects, such as music, to the present to maintain *straight* narratives of the nation makes me consider how dominant ideas of space and time feed traditional ways to represent who we are in a specific place (Allon, 2000). In other words, by using specific rituals and predominant traditions as the available options to narrate us, we comply with dominant ways to live space and time. This is political because "in order to be intelligible, we need to repeat the familiar and normalized" (Lather, 2007, p. 39). In many ways, this participant is no longer able to tell straight narratives about her "origins" back in Turkey. As she moves on her narratives, she becomes "original" in the United States (Rajchman, 1999). As Ahmed (2000) suggests, "The movements of subjects between places that come to be inhabited as home involve the discontinuities of personal biographies and wrinkles in the skin" (p. 91). Interestingly, she is not really clear about the reasons why she is bringing artifacts such as music and food to become part of her present in a different territory. She is extending a version of Turkey to her present as a way to explain her strangeness in a country different from her own. As Manning (2003) comments, "the image of the home as an extension of the nation surfaces often" (p. xvii). This participant expresses her confusion about not knowing why is it that she chooses to embrace an unquestioned nationalism that back in Turkey is not appealing to her. This drives her to narrate her experience of being *away* through nostalgic languages that reinforces ideas of the nation.

Later she continues,

> I don't know why I do it [to listen to Turkish music while in the U.S.]. Maybe I miss it because, you know, in Turkey is everywhere, I mean, you walk, you hear it at the shop, on TV. TVs are on all of the time. You know, you are overburdened with it. You don't want it but you hear the music, you know?

Home, wherever it is, is produced as the extension of the nation where nostalgia acts as a visceral impulse of our desire for attachment and belonging. In doing this, this participant refreshes a naturalized understanding of home that feeds a narrative of correspondence between bodies and territories. As she explains, the reasons why she insists on the idea of listening to Turkish music while in the United States, she constructs a negation of those cultural artifacts that may be a stereotype in the United States She thus states,

> Maybe it's the United States because you know, they do not have a long history. They don't have … okay, they have American things. They have dinners, they have their country music, they have, you know, they have all kinds of things, but when I compare it to Turkey there is so much history, there's so much variety in Turkey. You know various people, various cultures, sub-cultures.

I emphasize the idea of *things* that belong to a territory and the notion of time associated to territories; certain places look older than others and contain *more* cultures, identities, artifacts, and traditions.[2] It is interesting to read her way of justifying that her nationalistic impulses may have come from the fact that being in the country where she is makes these feelings *happen*, they become real. In this case, it is important to pay attention to what is at stake when this participant recognizes herself as a person who "belongs" to a specific territory and who is affected by the conditions imposed on the ways she narrates herself in a different territory. The political dynamics she creates around ideas of belonging, nation, and strict relations between identities and territories deserve attention since they are created out of dominant imaginaries of time and space that act behind our backs.

As I move through these narratives I see nostalgia as the dominant way in which we negotiate space and time. When we feel nostalgic about a time and a space left behind we begin to reconstruct and refine the vocabularies of nation, culture, and identity within our personal circles of experiences. Dancing, music, and food become the recognizable components of a space that tells things about who we are in a different country. They make us intelligible entities. It documents and legitimates our strangeness. It is the past with its objects that impels us toward the possibility of legitimizing strangeness. Bringing objects and practices owned by a specific territory to the narrative of being an "outsider" legitimizes the present position. As Elizabeth Grosz (2005) contends, "the past is contemporaneous with the present it has been. They exist, they 'occur' at the same time. The past and present are created simultaneously" (p. 103).

In a different set of conversations with my participant from Turkey, she talked about the ways she understood *other worlds* and how people inhabit them. For instance, I asked her whether she envisioned a place that was not good for her to travel and she replied, "...Umm, where there is war, or where there is...this is nothing ethnically or nothing personally, but I really would feel afraid of me going to Africa...I am afraid of animals." Again, the idea of territory filled with objects that may look unhealthy, dangerous, and strange provides us with orientations to think about places and our relations to them. It gives us a "particular mode of proximity" (Ahmed, 2000, p. 13) to them. For instance, my informant later narrated an encounter with some friends from Europe; the conversation was about them going to Turkey. According to her, one friend commented, "I am a blonde girl. I have blue eyes. I don't feel comfortable going to Turkey. You know, what they will do to us?" Territories have specific skin colors, feelings, and objects. The ways individuals orient themselves to those objects will define the experiences they may live in that territory.

Thus far, I have explored how movement serves to continue imagining nations and identities as organic and pure entities. Through these narratives I have presented how nostalgic impulses put to work dominant ways of understanding space and time. In many ways, these experiences of dislocation entail a way to orient our experiences to a time (past) and a space (away) that has effects on the ways we live, reside in the present. It is through these processes that "bodies take shape" (Ahmed, 2006, p. 2). Turkey has taken a specific shape so let's now explore Kenya's contours and how they are shaped through the other participant's narratives.

A KENYAN MALE NARRATIVE OF SPACE

Similar to the Turkish woman, this participant chose to talk about the meanings of belonging to a region through dancing, theater, and music. Related to these ideas, he stated the following:

I also miss a lot literature and entertainment which is unique to that region [Kenya] which I don't see here, like music, theater and all that. I just have had to cope with the types of theater and music I found here. Occasionally, I have tried to obtain the music or theatre of that type to bring here and see how it works. Yeah, so really I miss the whole environment and I also miss, like the general environment, like the vegetation and all that stuff. Here is different from at home, so what one would say that scenic value, the scenic value in my country being different from here. While I acknowledge being able to experience new scenic value, I also miss the value I'm used to.

A value is attached to what land can offer, which shapes not only how we inhabit space, but how we apprehend the present in the lack of *something*. He continues, "... But I also grew up in a mountainous region where things like tea, coffee are grown. All those mountains, plus tea and coffee are things you can never see here." To depict territories as perpetual (either because of their beauty or productivity) is a way to express the communal desire to preserve the intact cohesion between the one who narrates and those attributes related to richness, extravagance, and uniqueness of place. The official cultural texts of nations become embedded in the participants' narratives. For instance, what the interviewee mentions is a way to depict Kenya as a harmonious entity, in the same way as the participant from Turkey, where readers can see a clear scene of either Turkey or Kenya through the transparency of those experiences he narrates. As Manning (2003) contends, "The vocabulary of the nation can be understood as the structuring of a language that produces the distinction between qualified and unqualified bodies, where qualification within the identity and territory of the nation presupposes an attachment to the nation in its linguistic, cultural, and political incarnations" (p. xv). It is under this register that nostalgia comes to solidify an idea of coherence, of reinscription of already defined narratives of movement.

In a different conversation with the participant from Kenya, he constructed the idea of how gendered and sexualized cultures organize movement in Kenya. Gender and sexuality, as politics, exceed the space of the nation, as he explained,

> For women it is still [hard to study abroad], it doesn't really become an issue if a family learn that a man from the family is going to study abroad, but it is I think an issue when it is a woman, so you will have to beat the odds of family. If she's unmarried things may be slightly better for her, but if she's married, it is really difficult, I have seen some women who have turned down offers like that because of their family is likely to break. But typically a man is the one who is going abroad, it seems not to be an issue like that.

I argue that gender acts as a political technology to install the "naturalness" and unproblematic nature of movement in this student's narrative. A disembodied practice of movement as the one narrated by him means that a woman is the subject of vigilance in the home, of the heterosexual order, of monogamy, and this disembodied practice has effects on the ways ideas are reinscribed (e.g., ideas about who is entitled to produce knowledge).[3] This orients the conversation to a critical discussion where the "interest-laden nature of knowledge" and its connections to gender and heterosexuality are not acknowledged as a relevant dimension in the construction of "international" subjectivities and their production. This theme will be more fully developed in chapter seven.

In the same interview, the participant expresses,

> The woman is the home-maker and she cannot go out because there is always the worry of promiscuity when the woman is involved, more than when the man is concerned. But mostly because polygamy is really not advised in Africa and Kenya. Like in my country, the status quo does not allow polygamy, but there is also customary law, which allow, which has a constitutional acceptance, and it accepts polygamy.

Distance and movement evolve into nostalgia to secure women and heterosexuality in such a way that they subordinate themselves through the discourse of the strict order of the family. The production of a future for women is uncontained in this student's narratives. Women under patriarchal models are kept in the past itself. This scene becomes animated by dominant narratives of international movement.

He continues describing the ways Kenyan women struggle with the idea of autonomous travelling, "…sometimes the women themselves show reluctance when it comes to going away and leaving their family, because they know that it is possible and it is allowed that when the man remains behind he will get married again, and, but he will not devote her all the same." The uses of gender and sexuality to prevent a future for women in international education narratives require a problematization of the uses of dominant ways to enact space and time. A linear sense of time and the illusion that spaces contain bodies and objects marginalizes the political dimension on international students' representations of space and time and how one locates oneself and the others. These final thoughts provided by this participant captured the power involved in a nostalgic account of space and time. These thoughts evidence how the uses of dominant links of place and identity have specific effects in the organization of movement around gender and sexuality. The relationship among places, times, and bodies appear self-evident through nostalgia.

KEEP ME THERE—AN ACTIVE NOSTALGIA

Nostalgic pronouncements of who we are in relation to specific places and times act as a way to track cultural practices and social orders. In this way, caricatures of nations and feelings of *being away* organize our politics of separation and strangeness.

A reflection on the connection of the languages of nostalgia and nation is required to better understand the ways in which "the nation's very semantic structures" (Manning, 2003, p. xvi) work to perpetuate ideas of movement, of inhabiting, and becoming.

Susan Stewart (cited in Atia and Davies, 2010, p. 182) describes nostalgia as "sadness without an object." She takes us to a place where the nation, as an invention or container of subjectivities, privileges specific ways to be understood as a citizen; it takes us back to the idea of the "unreal" and the ways we construct interpretations about who we are from a fictitious correspondence between space and identity. International education discourses use nostalgia to produce an ideal construction of nation and its inhabitants as a model for the idea of a "diverse community." To secure Turkishness and Kenyanness through the language of nostalgia, participants need to invest in productions of Turkishness and Kenyanness, to cite just two examples, through multiple reiterations of defined relations to the territory, most of the time with no recognizable reasons. In other words, this is "an active nostalgia that is something more than just a rhetorically powerful propaganda technique. Equally, it is not simply a rational judicious preference for something lost over what remains" (Atia and Davies, 2010, p. 183). The repetitive enactment of nostalgia[4] has become naturalized to the extent that the collective memories of the nation, symbols, and rituals come to signify *the quintessential way* to narrate movement.

What is particularly relevant in the case of nostalgia associated with movement in the context of internationalization is that it serves "as a negotiation between continuity and discontinuity" (Atia and Davies, 2010, p. 184). In this case, continuity with what you bring as a member a different and distant community; and discontinuity to whatever the present has to offer. As Ahmed (2010) proposes,

> Nostalgia involves affective conversion. [It] is an affective state that resists the presence of a happy object that is no longer or that imagines something as being happy insofar as it is no longer. Things can be happy not only as projections of the future but also as imaginings of what has been lost. (p. 241)

While nostalgia has been a major driving force in constructing the international space in universities, the presence of nostalgia has been naturalized through the uses of dominant ways of thinking about space and time. Nostalgia acts as a demand of institutional discourses to preserve distinctive traits and to secure in advance that international bodies will look like "domestic bodies" in the future. To execute nostalgia through the imagining of objects and bodies who belong to specific territories overlaps with the reinvention of a sense of time in the cultural politics of universities. As bodies are constructed in policies, a sense of pregiven identity is asserted.

By presenting the analyses of the institutional documents and those of the international students narratives I not only demonstrated how "institutions provide collective [and] public spaces" (Ahmed, 2006, p.132), but also how we are limited in our ways of imagining ways to become fully constituted subjects through preexisting notions of time and space. Time and space, as we know them, cohere to form the contours of our experiences.

CHAPTER 3

MOVING BODIES—HOW DO WE DO TIME AND SPACE

In this chapter, I present the narratives of four graduate international students' stories from different countries and completing graduate degrees in the United States. These are stories of everyday lives and everyday encounters, and how they play out in the formation of social and institutional space and time in a US university. Here, the idea of experience becomes relevant when theorizing about time and space. Experience allows me to think about the ways dominant understandings of time and space fix ideas of who we are, the social and cultural positions we occupy. And, they frame the expectations and orientations we should follow. To pay attention to the ways embodied subjectivities are put to work for these students within the institutional language of the international is vital to understanding the ways such discourses go against the complexities students face as gendered, classed, and raced subjects. The ways in which they narrate and locate experience in relation to time and space are vital for examining the complexities of internationalization discourses. To ignore the embodied nature of knowledge that this group of people produce can reflect the interested nature of one type of educational prescription embedded in internationalization discourses.

The role that time and space play in the production of institutional academic subjectivities is relevant. Space as empty and time as linear facilitates the operation of other conceptualizations such as success, nation, and progress. I am interested in how the ideas of time and space are exercised in narratives of movement told by international graduate students. The invocation of students' images of the past, the emotions involved in the retelling and the frustrations, fears, and silences of the present make their stories relevant for questioning who they have become and how they might relate to other ways of fixation. They also make possible a critique of the particular educational prescriptions that internationalization discourses promote. In other words, I tell the stories of personal traveling to seek how dominant constructions of space and time play out in the ways we narrate ourselves. I think that the possibility to work with people who are in transit between territories is particularly relevant. It provides a context to theorize "ways to tell ourselves" with certain unique characteristics. Being aware of being a *body in motion* provides the possibility to complicate experience as a subjectified body. Academics moving around the world are aware of being positioned in a different location than that of their origin; they are aware of themselves as *bodies in motion*. Therefore, it becomes natural for them to be aware of the ways discourses provide possibilities for them to be read as a specific kind of body. It is when one is "outside" (whatever that means) that one becomes conscious of the ways your privilege (or lack of privilege) works. All of a sudden, your skin color, your gendered and sexed politics become possibilities or obstacles to narrate what is going on. These stories are to be contrasted with those other stories told from the experiences of regulation and monitoring. Both provide different scenes of the same body recognizing herself on a specific time and space.

Through conversations I seek to understand the images of time and space international students use to tell their stories. As I have suggested throughout the book, time and space operate as forces that act behind our backs, as political dimensions from where other selves may be possible to be told. When narrating experiences of "returning" and "going to," ideas of time and space are particularly visible and important possibilities to express and qualify experiences. To "move" provides a way to experience our relation to time and space that are more evident in our stories. Some of these intensities to tell the story of movement resonate across all the four participants. There are others that diverge, revealing specific contradictions and problematic connections to who they are, where they come from, and where they find themselves now. As the following paragraphs suggest, the stories that unfold in this chapter are unique in their combinations of aspects of personal, political, and intellectual lives of each of the four international students.

In this chapter, I begin with a brief introduction of four international students describing their academic and social backgrounds. They come from different countries, which can be read as a territorial reading of the United States and its politics to produce places, times, and bodies. I pay special attention to how Japan, Turkey, Kenya, and Colombia may be understood not only as accomplished projects of nationhood and citizenship but also as political possibilities of distance and cultural production of institutional spaces in the United States Countries, in this case, do not stand before people, they are sites of possibilities to become outsiders or insiders. In both scenarios, there is a way to understand and give meanings to the very facts that create ourselves and our stories. I discuss how students' transition process from "home" to the United States has been lived by them. I focus much of my discussion on how ideas of experience as a space to narrate and time to fragment life become a relevant element in theorizing who they were and who they may become. Experience, in this case, is conceived as the meeting point of particular and contingent ideas of time and space. As I have said earlier, this discussion is illustrated by quotes from the participants, theories related to the main issues discussed, and my own personal thoughts. The linkage of these various elements facilitate a more complex telling of those lives of students presented in this chapter and chapter four.

ACTUAL BODIES

Ann is a Turkish international student whose area of study is Curriculum and Instruction. She has been at the University for almost four years. Her academic experience in her home country was defined by her work in a university known for being particularly *westernized*. This institution was founded by a group of missionaries from the United States around 1850. It was initially established as a high school, then it became a Turkish state university. For many Turkish people, this university upholds US American traditions within

Turkey. All courses are taught in English and most of the professors in her department have received their higher education in the United States. There are four universities of this type in Turkey; the one Ann attended is state-run. Having been a student at such an institution in Turkey made Ann feel as if her experiences as a student in the United States would not be much different from those she had in Turkey. She completed her master degree and then started working as a research assistant for three years there. She emphasized in the interviews that her position as a research assistant was never important and that it involved primarily more administrative than research duties. At that time she was single and came to the United States by herself. She was under J-1 visa status, which means that she was studying with funding from the Turkish government. We had known each other since 1999 and all our meetings took place in her apartment.

Javiera is from Colombia and has been living in the United States since 2001. She is a lawyer by profession who took an interest in the field of education because she had been teaching beginner lawyers in her country for 12 years. She had also worked as a lawyer in a professional firm, but her desire and interest in education made her consider academia as the place that could best fulfill her aspirations. In Colombia, her academic work focused more on teaching than research. Her choice of teaching—as opposed to research—had to do with the dynamics of the university where she worked. It is a private institution where the central activity is teaching; research is a peripheral activity that faculty may choose to in addition to teaching activities. Her university is an elite institution; it is one of the most expensive institutions in Colombia. Thus, the student body belongs mostly to the upper classes. At the time of the interviews, Javiera was a full-time faculty member there. She was living in the United States with her husband who is from Spain. She initially arrived in this country by herself and was then joined by her husband. She was a Fulbright student. Every year that she had been in the United States she returned to Colombia during the summer break to teach classes at her university.

Peter is from Kenya and came to the United States in 2001. He has a wife and two children, an eight- and a two-year-old boy at the time of the interviews. During his time in the United States, Peter's family was in Kenya. He completed a master's degree in Kenya in the area of Curriculum Development and mainly focused on methods of teaching social sciences, specifically history and geography. He has been a faculty member at the university in Kenya since 1996. In Kenya, he was involved in both research and teaching. His research focused on the ways educational programs address the needs of teachers, children, and individual schools. Peter's research used mostly action research methodology since in Kenya his duties were oriented mostly to the monitoring and evaluation of different educational programs. He designed instruments of evaluation, administered them, and finally analyzed his findings to present them to different commissions and policy-related meetings. These were long-term projects so when he left Kenya to come to the United States, they were continued by his successors. His university is a private one, which differs from public institutions as far as funding is concerned, but is alike in terms of the way their programs are administered. It is one of the top private universities even though public universities are often ranked higher than private ones in Kenya. Recently, and because of new policies targeting private universities, the reputation of his institution had improved because its student–teacher ratio was lower than those in public universities. He is a Fulbright visitor scholar and holds a J-1 visa.

Sarah is from Japan. She used to live in a different state in the United States before coming to her current university setting. Her husband was about to complete his Master's degree in that state when they decided to move and complete their Ph.D degrees elsewhere in the United States. She majored in History and her only chance for a professional career in Japan was to become a teacher. Since she was required to pay a very large sum of money to become a teacher, she preferred to use this money to do something else. She studied English and applied for a job in a transnational company. While she was studying English she met her husband with whom she began thinking about coming to the United States. At the beginning, her plan was to come to this country by herself to study English. While her husband was completing his Master degree in the US, she decided to begin her graduate studies. She covered the majority of the expenses during her first year from her own pocket. She came from a middle-class family so she and her husband were able to support themselves for a period of time. She does not have professional connections or ties to any university back in Japan, so her situation is quite different from the other three. She is under the F-1 visa status. Her financial support comes from her family and from her on-campus graduate assistantship work.

While the four international students have many experiences and background in common, Sarah's account was different in many aspects. First, the fact of being under a different visa category gives her some greater liberties in relation to the other three participants. For instance, she is not forced to leave the country after completing her degree. Her relationship to her home country is also different from the other participants' who are primarily J-1 students. During the interview process, I found that she, like the other participants, went through an equally intense emotional process upon arriving in the United States. I would say that her situation in terms of professional stability is more complicated than the other three participants. Being connected to an academic institution in home countries makes the return process to these countries easier, and at the same time universities occupy a position of power in that they can force students to come back. Sarah will need to find a job either in Japan or the United States, which may not be an easy task for an international student.

These people left their homes on their own to come to a distant and foreign place for their education. Most are here for that purpose alone, fully intending and required by their visas to return to their home after graduation. One way to read these experiences is that the major motivation of each of these students in coming to the United States to study is travel across countries and continents to encounter a different culture and educational system based on premises that diverge widely from their own. One can expect that each of these students must therefore create important new ways of living these experiences; they must explore differences in values, beliefs and practices in ways that call for complex disruptive processes of displacement and belonging. Nonetheless, I argue that the conceptualizations of space and time we use provide a different status to the experience of an outsider. This is a way to understand how it is to live as a body that is constantly being differentiated from other bodies. Focusing on ideas of correspondence to a specific place and how that place belongs to a different time (usually the past), we can see how the experience of "the outsider" comes to be organized.

I think the experience of becoming an international student provides a space where borders and dreams become ruptured, blurred, and undefined. However, because of the ways we have been told to use concepts of time and space to make sense of our movement and practices of inhabiting places, we create a narration of attachment, belonging, and location where geographies, nations, and bodies become resources to recount and justify the effects of moving. Being oriented only to movement can be disturbing. So, the only option is to improvise; improvise identity and improvise ways to relate to values. Being a subject always in flux (imaginarily or materialistically speaking) displaces the very notion of identity, particularly within the context of globalization. In other words, the images of stability and the strict correspondence with the social and cultural position we occupy are put into question when the experience of movement is placed at the center.

On the other hand, the idealistic image of these *bodies in motion* are used by the liberal agenda of globalization in higher education to promote and intensify notions of correspondence and stability of identities and territories, sustain the disembodiment and subsequent impossibility for these people to narrate their stories, and promote the neutral aspect of knowledge production. Since stability in terms of a clean, fixed correspondence to a territory and the dominant notion of time that frames home as in-the-past are taken for granted, bodies as in-motion, or in flux, appear extraordinary. Therefore, students' accounts that maintain notions of stability or fixed presence play an important role in inciting the liberal agenda of globalization. The idea of the mobile intellectual allows a certain privilege to operate. It is almost like the future is that of a scholar who conquered the world. As important as it is to have these possibilities to imagine oneself, I argue that these experiences of movement can be told in many ways. No doubt that imagining themselves as subjects *in motion* helps them shape who they are in a range of considerable ways.

What the interviews illuminate is the sequential way to narrate the journey. Therefore, displacement is the common tone and pulse of these stories. The self is represented in a range of conflicting and conflicted ways. My intention is to enable the reader to get into these subjects' stories and become part of them. Moreover, I seek to reveal how international students mediate the past, present, and future in different contexts. Besides presenting their own voices embedded in excerpts, I intend to provide theoretical elements to illuminate and complicate their stories. My purpose is to offer a more complex and multilayered account of their lives.

I believe that their stories deserve a more complex and multileveled understanding of the practices of times and spaces and the ways these conceptualizations, when they are presented in their dominant discourses, affect the chances they have to position and imagine themselves. This understanding can potentially respond to, complicate, and broaden a simple identity politics framework that assumes the self as static and rooted to a single community and territory. The experiences and narratives of the students are not only full of feelings of isolation, frustration, and self-sacrifice but also of sentiments of happiness and accomplishment. The cultural, social, and racial relativism that results from their displacement opens up new worlds for them. This is what I find so inspiring in their sometimes moving and often painful narratives.

REGULATING THE STRANGE AND SOMEHOW DANGEROUS BODY

It is my purpose in this chapter to discuss the narratives produced because of the institutional processes international students undergo when deciding to come to the United States. I pay special attention to the ways time and space can open up possibilities to narrate specific conceptualizations of who people are and who they may become. Retheorizing time and space permits a reading of experience that challenges globalization, and notions of internationalization of higher education. There is extensive literature that addresses the particular processes international students follow when deciding to study abroad.[1] Beyond an explanation of the process itself, I want the reader to capture the elements that provide a sense of how different discourses regulate the creation of specific experiences to be lived by international students from the very beginning of their journey.

Most of the time, the process of applying for admission and scholarships to universities starts one year before the individual actually arrives in the United States. The period spent doing interviews, paperwork, tests, can be discouraging for many prospective applicants. For instance Javiera (Colombia) recalls this process:

> Yes, the idea to start the process one year ahead, they use your time, and the attitude of these people is like "you want something that we have, so you have to be available at our time, and do it the way we say it." They call you at the middle of the afternoon and tell you "you have to come to get a document" like one has nothing better to do than just to wait for them to call.

In a different conversation we discussed the types of questions asked during the interviews, how they were constructed, and what was the purpose underlying them. Most of the participants expressed the complicated situation they experienced when being interviewed by different people during the process of applying to US universities. Javiera (Colombia) recounted the following:

> Yes, the interviews were very intimidating. Particularly I remember once that the first question they asked me was something along the lines of describing in detail the program I wanted to attend in U.S. It seemed to me that the person was trying to get some information that he did not know about, I mean, he was not a lawyer. What details was he expecting? I remember myself once applying for a master in commercial law and the person who was interviewing me wanted me to give him details of a program in commercial law, when he was not even a lawyer and was not going to understand what I was talking about.

Ann (Turkey) also recalls her experience when being interviewed:

> There were four or five professors, they asked me questions I really thought were unrelated. They asked me what I think about the States, the United States' policy with Cuba or something else, American long-time policy for history, you know, weird questions. They asked whether I went back to Turkey, or if I would want to work in a university in the Eastern part of Turkey, you know, these types of questions.

The processes under which international students are monitored start from the moment they decide to go to the United States. It is relevant to underscore how the process itself starts with the assumption that for whatever reason, international students could be *dangerous* to the country's well-being. Within the framework of international education and considering the high economic value assigned to international students in the United States, it is important to look at and consider the reasons why international students decide to come to this country. The United States is seen as a place where international students can obtain a better education and experience for their professional careers. For instance, in the case of Ann (Turkey), it is relevant to look at how her decision to come to the United States was inspired by her previous *western* experience in Turkey. When asked why she decided to come to the United States to study she says:

> Anyway, I think my university education affected me [in terms of my decision to come to U.S.]. And also, I think it affected me because, you know, most of my professors came from the States, not from England, and also, you know, I lived in Europe for a couple of years. I kind of know what Europe is like. Maybe I didn't [want to go back to Europe], I wanted to see the States.

Sarah (Japan) also had something to say about why she chose the United States:

> Do I have to [explain why I came to the U.S.]? I mean do I need to answer that? No, no, I mean it is so obvious, like if you want to study abroad, the U.S. is the first place that you want to look at. And it's like more prestigious if you get a Ph.D in U.S. than in another country.

The reasons to come to the United States seem particularly interesting considering that after the events of September 11, 2001, in the United States most of the international students are seen or thought as terrorist who need to prove the contrary. But these regulations do not only affect the universities; these regulations also have an impact on the lives and processes regulating international students while they are in United States. It is true that they may not influence the decisions of students coming to the United States but once international students are in United States the consequences of these regulations in regard to their daily lives are considerable.

SECURITY, NATION, AND AFFECT

When talking about the ways regulations after September 11, 2001, operates to justify monitoring and create a sense of insecurity for international students, I saw that the participants displayed a certain degree of anxiety created by the increased monitoring in the past years. For instance, Peter (Kenya) made a case for how his civil liberties have been compromised by the new policies and how they affect the way he himself relates to the United States and the world:

INTERVIEWER: Do you think that the September 11 events have affected your stay in the US?

PETER: Yes, you see there are two ways I feel it. One, is that you cannot even express your ideas about international politics at this point in a really free manner, because you don't know how it is perceived here by citizens of the United States.

INTERVIEWER: But, is this because you are an *international student*?

PETER: Yes, because we may not share exactly the same views as them. We may have different views, which are not necessarily subversive to the United States, but they certainly don't go over well with them. That is just one side of the explanation, like I have two positions, so that is just one. Because we are not citizens of the United States we may not share the national feelings, the exact national feelings, the citizens of this country have towards their nation. And, it is possible that they may not see it in that perspective, that we have as well been patriotic to our own, wherever you came from, originally. I'm not taking the higher moral ground necessarily, that being an international student I have now been able to, if different countries becomes that's who I am, it's likely experienced at a different level. I'm just talking about the simple fact of patriotic, that my national feelings are different from their national feelings, because the nation to which my allegiance is paid, is different from theirs. And we certainly have different ideas. So, from a very honest point of view, honest in the sense that I am being patriotic to my country, and they are being patriotic to theirs, we might probably both agree on ways of looking at things.

Peter also makes a relevant point when talking about feelings of insecurity while in the United States:

> PETER: I have never felt secure here despite the fact that this could be the perfect nation in the world, but I've never felt safer here the way I feel at home. When I am among those many Africans and people and my relatives, all that group, the sense of security there is...
>
> INTERVIEWER: Yes, it's different.
>
> PETER: Yes, and despite the fact that the police system [in Kenya] may not be as good as it is here, but the sense of security I feel when I'm there is higher. The sense of confidence, the sense of belonging. Here I just feel like a foreigner, you know? That kind of thing.
>
> INTERVIEWER: Yes, and do you think that this feeling is caused by the problems that they have here with racial issues? Or it is just a combination of issues?
>
> PETER: The other one [referring to his sense of displacement], as I said earlier on, is purely environmental, climatic condition. And then the second one has to do with the rights and liberties that I can access here and that I can say all those give a sense of security.
>
> When I'm at home, I know I can speak and demand my rights like this is my country. What will you do? You have to do this for me, all that. But here you, you take only what you are given. If you are told you can't work, you really can't do that.

The sense of insecurity and fear belongs to specific ideas of time and space. As Peter was describing his experiences of being an outsider, we see "fear [play out as] an embodied experience" (Ahmed, 2004, p. 68). Fear and feeling unsafe tells about a specific way to relate to space and time.[2] We might consider this fear a regulation in that its effect, feeling insecure and unsafe, "works to contain some bodies such that they take up less space" (Ahmed, 2004, p. 69).

Moving to a different example, ways that define the monitoring of the experiences of international students are more implicit. In terms of economic profit to the universities, graduate international students serve many of the universities' purposes at a low cost. For instance, they contribute to the viability of many teaching programs and research projects, especially in the sciences. If universities and the US government understand that international students come to the United States to pursue studies and because of regulations they are not allowed to stay in this country, arbitrarily monitoring and regulating students' lives while temporarily in the United States becomes easier.

In relation to academia and how international students experience their university lives, it is important to look at the ways they talk about their frustrations and how, in many ways, their experiences in the United States do not take into account their previous academic and intellectual backgrounds. Moreover, the systematic omission or erasure of who they are in their home countries profoundly affects their experiences in the United States. To erase one's previous experiences produces negation, which in many ways is taken on by the subject as a sign of her or his own invisibility and resentment.

Javiera (Colombia) makes an interesting point regarding these matters:

INTERVIEWER: How would you describe your relation with the faculty, broadly speaking?

JAVIERA: In general, I feel myself welcomed as an international student who comes for a short time and leaves. I mean, I had this idea since I came here. For instance, there is a sentence I hear constantly, I know that it is important to have in mind the length of my scholarship and fulfill the deadlines within the program.

INTERVIEWER: To go back home as soon as you can?

JAVIERA: Exactly, it is like, "I am going to help you to do what you have to do and leave when you have to leave. And if you have funding for three years, organize yourself to do what you have to do in these three years." So as long as my intentions are not different from this, I feel myself welcomed. If you want to do something else, then you do not receive enough support, for instance, to publish, to get support to do academic stuff, if you want to do some other type of research, or if you want to explore a professional opportunity, then you feel yourself completely left to your own devices. I have felt a lot of support from professors, but it is in academic terms, like "your paper is good and it is a pleasure to read it and make comments on it," but it is not more than that.

The feeling of detachment and disengagement from academia affects international students. It is produced by a strong need of the university to comply with its internationalization goals and to identify international students as specific subjects. The university provides space as long as "one stays correctly in time. The unstated order is about a moral use of time oriented around being productive" (Sharma, 2014, p. 144).[3]

When Javiera (Colombia) spoke about this idea of being named as a student, it is interesting to see the ways in which it affects her perception of herself. She says:

JAVIERA: Yes, let's say that to me, the first time I came here it was a big shock to see myself treated as a *student*. To be considered as a *student*, after twelve years of being a professional. It was like a process of assimilation to realize that here I am not a professor, I am not a director of a department, none of that. I am a student, a graduate student and that simply means a student who is in a program called *graduate*. I believe that that was a process that I had to go through and at the end I like it because of what it means in terms of relaxation.

INTERVIEWER: Relaxation?

JAVIERA: Yes. If a person comes from one of our home countries, seeing herself as a professional, and enrolls in a university and tries to keep living a professional life, well I think that person will be living against the system. I agree. I agree with the idea that delivering papers in conferences and publishing articles will be part of our professional development, not only to develop student activities. It would be interesting to have those possibilities and to have support to carry them out. But that support is not here. But let's say that I do understand that in a system like this we are students, simply students. For instance, this was very peculiar because the last class I attended in legal education, the topic was diversity. They prepared an exercise to identify the persons next to you, on both sides and you had to use just one word to identify the person beside you. I had the two professors from the class on both sides. One of them called me *graduate* and the other one identifies me as *foreigner*. And the two of them told me that they would have called me either graduate student or foreign student, but they only could use one word. So this is what defines you. I would have said

Colombian and then we did not talk about the issue. But this identification determines a lot of what you can do here and what you cannot.

INTERVIEW: How does the fact of being named as a foreigner make you feel?

JAVIERA: Everything and nothing. It is not something I perceive all the time. I never feel myself fully integrated to the classroom for instance where I was telling you about the activity where all the classmates are US students except me. [This feeling of foreignness/ detachment is something] I perceived all the time so it did not mean anything to me that they called me that in that classroom. Besides, I am auditing this class, so I do not feel myself part of the class. The auditing student category contributes to that feeling of detachment.

The public experience of being denied opens up a possibility to talk about the uses of institutional space and time by the "western subject" and how the foreigner becomes silenced. In a different paragraph, Javiera (Colombia) notes,

JAVIERA: I want to add one thing that I think it is cultural and it is the American egocentrism. In some ways, they do not believe you have anything to teach them.

INTERVIEWER: But do you perceive this idea coming from the professors?

JAVIERA: From everybody. My feeling is that, the fact of you being a professional with academic experience in your home country is not relevant to them because they think there is nothing in your country or from your experience that enriches theirs. It is as if they've always invented everything therefore their system works perfectly. They think that you live in a country where people kill each other so what can you possible say about democracy or teaching or how to educate a child? We know that more than anybody in the world.

INTERVIEWER: And how do you see this issue in opposition to the multicultural rhetoric at the university?

JAVIERA: [They say] "international students enrich the university a lot."

INTERVIEWER: Exactly. It is like they are proud of having international students.

JAVIERA: No I think this is not true. I believe that we are a blessing for them just as long as having international students brings status for the university. One day, professor X told me something along these lines in his class. There were I don't know what number of international students. I told him that in many of my classes at the college the minorities were US students and he replied to me: "Can you believe this? And we have never had a meeting to discuss the meaning of this. I mean, if this is the composition of the college of education today, there would be some educational policies."

As I move through these lines, the notions of how space "contains" experiences, people, and ideas is appealing. The idea that places are particular fragments of a bigger picture, and that they contain all the particularities of the master narrative can be unpacked. The university as a particular place "containing" purified notions of "people from different countries," constructs international students' identities to fit within an already established realm of possibilities that are configured as stable and fixed. To stabilize international students' identities affect or certain kind of affection is required. Affect becomes the mechanism through which international students explore experiences that do not look quite rewarding. Universities become a space of international students to forcefully claim an identity through emotions of denial and fear. It is through these feelings that "nation" comes into existence as a source of security and safety.

The relation between identity and experience is an important one, which I will now discuss in more depth. Some theorists, arguing against identity politics, have charged that *experience* is not a self-evident or even reliable source of knowledge, and cannot be used to ground social identity (Moya and Hames-García, 2000). This notion of identity is foregrounded in specific ways to understand time and space. For instance, to believe that identity is self-evident implies the recognition that social and cultural positions are possible and reliable. This requires stabilized, fixed, solid, unchanging ideas of time as linear and space as empty. Thus, the location of identities within time and space becomes unproblematic. Postmodernists point out that personal experiences are essentially unstable and slippery, and, since they can only be interpreted in terms of linguistic or other signs, they must rely on individual interpretation and therefore are replete with ideology as they are accompanied by social identification (Moya and Hames-García, 2000, p. 31). This constructed nature of identity shows why "there is no guarantee that a person's experiences will lead to some common core of values or beliefs that link that person with another member of the same group" (Rodriguez, 2000, p. 155, cited in Petrunic, 2005). If we complicate time and space in the ways we tell experience, we will have a particular understanding of what we can expect, dream, or fight for. As Joan Scott (1991) states, "experience is a linguistic event that does not happen outside established meanings" (p. 793). Accordingly, experience cannot be understood apart from language, and since language is a social and historical creation, "historical processes through discourse, position subjects and produce their experiences" (p. 779). Scott claims, "we can understand the processes that produce these discourses and produce the experiences of difference itself" (p. 793).

So, I will consider experience as an interpretation, something produced. International students therefore interpret what is an "experience" to them and in so doing they construct themselves. In this case, what we name as an experience is no more than "the 'invention' of [the international student]" (Britzman, 2000, p. 31). Thus, the discourses that name and describe the international student become viewed as synonymous with experience, as Deborah Britzman (2000) notes when talking about the production of the student teacher. Experience cannot have meaning on its own. This implies that all the categories of identity—racial, sexual, national, and so on—are the products of historically specific discourses, where the categories are limited to these discourses and function to historicize the experience they mediate (Moya and Hames-García, 2000, p. 275).

In graduate programs, curriculum also becomes an important vehicle to regulate and produce the experiences of international students at the university level. Javiera says:

[Once I came to U.S.] I thought that I could discuss on what I was doing in the classroom at the university in Colombia. There were times when I talked about my academic interests in Colombia, I have struggled to do it, but nobody seems interested in it. I tried to find a space for myself. For me this semester was almost traumatic because I was searching for a class that really interested me [a class that combines law and education]. I never expected to find a class at the college of law, because the profile of this university's college of law is totally oriented towards practice, the practice of law, particularly at the commercial level. I mean, the topics [discussed in the school of law] were not relevant to me, even in political or philosophical terms. Everything is geared toward technical knowledge on how to earn money; this is the philosophy of this place. Then I was always looking at the curriculum in a very lazy manner, and this semester when I discovered this seminar; they had started three weeks earlier and I went crazy with happiness to think that I was searching for a law professor interested in law education for almost two years. I had asked everybody I knew. When I discovered these two people I thought I was going to die of happiness and I showed up in their class the following day and I told them. I talked to her [the instructor of the class] first, then I talked to him [the other instructor]. I told them that I was a graduate student from the college of education but what I really was a law professor from Colombia with experience in active methods of teaching interested in active pedagogy in law education in the U.S. I emphasized that it "was be very important to attend the seminar" and the professor answered, "Interesting, let me talk to my colleague because this class is done by two professors, so send us an email." When the class was over I talked to the other professor, I told him exactly the same thing, the same rhetoric, and he told me, "that's fine I am going to talk to my colleague, send us an email." When I got home and talked to my husband I told him "maybe they did not understand me, I think this is because of my English. If I were one of them, if I were a professor I would be fascinated by the idea of having a professor from a different country interested in the same topic as myself, even I would have asked, "Can you give us a lecture?" I am not saying that they have to treat me as a colleague and divide the class in three (laughing), but, please give me something! I mean, I wouldn't have said, "wait I am going to talk to my colleague," like for decency yes, but you may say "let me introduce you X." I was thinking, "could it be that they did not understand me?" Then I sent them the email telling them everything very clearly, about my twelve years of experience, blah, blah, blah. At the end they replied, "we would like you to be with us as an auditing student. Feel free to participate when you want to, it is good that you provide your experiences." And I haven't opened my mouth, I tell you, all of them are young people. And there was a class all about teaching methods and I thought, "I am going to talk," but the whole class was about one method, and the class was over.

Then, I saw nobody interested in the methods we use in Colombia, nor did they ask me how I do this or that.

Similar ideas are common in different ways to all the participants. Moreover, all participants were very critical of the lack of attention to what really means to have international students in the graduate programs. Javiera (Colombia) continued her comments:

JAVIERA: I think that the comment from professor X is relevant because it made me realize that they, at the college of education, have never questioned what it means for them and for their educational practice to have international students in classes in large numbers. It means that they have to rethink classes in a different way, to integrate other topics, other texts, other readings, give a space to international students to talk about their experiences and also question themselves [the faculty] if they are interested in listening to international students. Let's open up a space for them to express themselves.

INTERVIEWER: I hope we are moving to that place.

JAVIERA: Then my question is in what ways do they enrich themselves with what international students do here on campus?

INTERVIEWER: Yes, how do they incorporate their experiences in the curriculum?

JAVIERA: Right, I think this would modify the curriculum and the classes we take. It would be very interesting to enroll in a class modified by those attending the class. Besides it is very funny because this is what they are telling you all the time [how to design relevant classes for the students].

Javiera (Colombia) also spoke about how all these experiences affected her own professional goals and expectations:

I believe that [a graduate international student is] a person who comes to enroll in classes, to fulfill the program and wants to go back to her/his home country. This person is seen as another student whose professional experience does not count in terms of what this person comes to do here. From the point of view of the international student, and in my case I also see myself like someone who is here temporarily who came to enrich herself with an academic experience and eventually to explore new tendencies in study and research that I couldn't have done back in my home country. But, professionally, I see myself in Colombia.

What this discussion shows is that there is a problem when students' identities are taken for granted since selves are produced and reproduced through social interactions, daily negotiations, and within the university context that is already overloaded with meanings about international students. If these are the types of criticisms provided by international students, it is critical to find a way to represent their questionings in order to improve their experience in the United States This should be carried out by favoring university academic processes over administrative or regulatory ones. In the case of international students, and especially for this book, the emphasis is on "the discourse of experience rather than experience itself"(Britzman, 1992, p.30). International students are the tellers of their experiences, but significantly, their potential to retell their stories is set by the conditions of discourse. Foucault (cited in McHoul and Grace, 1997) describes experience as "the correlation between fields of knowledge, types of normativity, and forms of subjectivity in a particular culture" (p. 27). In this version, experience is a sort of regulating fiction. As Britzman (1992) notes, "how one understands experience depends upon what it is that structures one's capacity to name something as experience in the first place. In naming something as an experience the *I* of that experience must also be produced, become intelligible" (p. 38). A poststructuralist approach to identity, then, is concerned "with tracing identity as subjected to the constraints of social structure to the practices of discourse. As discursive boundaries shift, so, too do identities" (Britzman, 1992, p. 28).

Our identities, overdetermined by history, place, and sociality, are lived and imagined through the discourses or knowledge we employ to make sense of who we are, who we are not, and who we may become. Identity, then, always signifies relationships to the other and consequently, as Chris Weedon (1999) asserts, must be negotiated. A poststructuralist position on subjectivity relativizes the individual's sense of self by making it an effect of discourse, which is open to a continuous redefinition that is constantly evolving. International students become vulnerable intellectuals who produce and are produced by culture, language, discourse, and the social positions they inhabit.

To trouble the relation among places, times, and subjectivities is a way to address the lived experiences of thousands of people who go abroad to pursue graduate studies. It permits a shift in the focus from where students come from toward one on where they are at (Gilroy,1991). Indeed places to be lived by people in transit are critically important because of the always-evolving interpretation and retelling of who they are in the very process of transition occurring in between and within places. One way to think about the relation of place, time, and identities is through the interpreting of the contradictions, silences, fears, and displacements of their experiences as a reaction to the several cultural assumptions embedded in places to inhabit by this group of people.

The sense of no longer feeling totally connected to a particular race, culture, language, or background represents a critical approach on how we understand the relation between identity and place (Massey, 1994). The question would be if narratives of displacement are able to deconstruct ideas about our senses of attachment and provoke particular ways academics question who they are and what they do.

What interests me about the stories told by international students is that by troubling stories about who they are in their countries, which is different from how they have been constructed in the United States, enables me to understand the conditions and uses to produce new subjectivities within contemporary universities.

CHAPTER 4

THE STRANGE BODY

As the figure of a person occupying a space not of her own, the figure of the stranger appears to represent the one who does not belong (Ahmed, 2000). In this chapter, I explore on how ideas of the *strange body* are produced in research studies and how these notions affect the ways we inhabit institutional spaces and times. To do this I explore on the discourses presented in research studies about international students and the ways they provide the contours by which to live and experience space and time. In this chapter, I present a discussion on the notion of the graduate international student as constructed by research studies in which the production of deficient subjects is a way to enforce the ideal notion of a person occupying a particular space and time in US educational institutions. Here, it is important to pay attention to the roles and operations of a disembodied identity that is produced in research studies. By disembodiment I mean the detachment of the body from the particularities of time and space (Bordo, 1986).[1] As *bodies in motion* are represented in research as lacking and culturally deficient, the image of the subject is of someone who can be read as neutral, absolute, and detached; detached from her/his "original space" and her/his tempos. This has important effects on the ways we recreate the idea of the exotic Other, containing all the attributes and dispositions of a community, expressing all the singularities of particular geographies, and belonging to the times of those spaces (as presented in chapter 2). Therefore, I argue that the production of particular subjects in research is an effect of particular ideas of space and time.

Disembodiment as a particular value to produce international students' identities requires ignoring the ways in which space and time shape people's stories of international movement. Here, I am saying that the ways research studies present the ideas of time and space then are in line with dominant notions, such as that space contains shared, recognizable experiences of unity, and time relates to the sequential understanding of development and progress. As such, time and space are relevant dimensions for the construction of social and cultural differentiation in institutions of higher education.

In different ways, research studies on international students act as a matrix where identities get mapped onto particular bodies and get aligned with particular times and spaces, in turn installing specific discursive arrangements and favoring particular arrangements of power. To produce this group of students as deficient and lacking requires the use of specific notions of time and space. For example, time as divisible to map social practices for international students is a way to attach them to particular characteristics. Space as static reinforces the unequal relations of insider–outsider. In other words, to think of developmental stages to position international students' experiences is a way to segment and differentiate dispositions and abilities for this group of people. As Sidhu and Dall'Alba (2012) note, "Deficit discourses, [. . .], are a useful rationalizing instrument to shift responsibility for ethnocentrism, including the reluctance to cater for students with diverse experience and lack of preparation for addressing the challenges of teaching international students" (p. 419). Moreover, to produce the deficient international student is an elegant way to justify marginalization and discrimination of those who are produced and imagined as outsiders. To explore on the ways research produces specific subjects we can trace how space and time are used to marginalize specific identities and practices. In other words, to practice space and time under particular circumstances is a way to politicize our institutional experiences.

The aim of this chapter and chapter three is to trace the invention of the international student through the research discourses that make them institutionally intelligible. What they narrate as the *experience* of being an international student is not more than the retelling of the process of invention of the international student (Britzman, 2000). By this I mean that their stories are full of passages where they construct who they are in relation to specific ideas of space, and narrate their trajectories within specific notions of time. Dominant notions of time and space then act as involuntary and powerful forces to construct oneself. The several levels produced and sustained in research to name international students, for example, "the student at risk" or "the student with language deficits," are possible through the reliance on specific notions of time and space. Time and space enable research to produce identities for international students as intelligible at least in two ways. First, as they *belong* to a different territory, therefore they are produced as different people (different from those domestic students). Second, as they are different bodies they are produced as in lack and deficit. With this image the asymmetric relations among "insider," "outsider," "black," "white," "man," "women" recover strength; these asymmetric relations become revitalized under the umbrella of internationalization of higher education. International students belong to specific geographies, they do not become (Massumi, 2002). Then, being a legitimate international student requires the performance of ways to occupy institutional spaces and times in particular manners.

Then, one question to organize this thinking would be, what if we were able to tell ourselves using other ways to imagine space and time? What other discursive possibilities would appear?

I now turn my attention to how research produce ways to naturalize the world for graduate international students and those who are named as domestic. Discrete subjects and objects of international space and time are produced through research that maintains a compensatory approach to produce international students, because of their condition of being *outsiders*. The challenge, therefore, is to question how particular knowledge incites specific ways to frame narratives, possibilities, and feelings that direct us to specific ways to relate to each other.

As research produces a specific way to imagine international students' identities, experiences, tastes, behaviors, feelings, and the like, policies also produce specific constructions of the international student. When policies are interpreted as discourses, issues of subjectivity become critically relevant to understand the web of possibilities for subjects seen as the Other (the international student, women, the immigrant, the refugee, etc.). The authoritative regulatory discourse of policies on international students in the United States, particularly after September 11, 2011, is a perfect scenario to view policies as cultural producers that condition experience, affect interpretation of who we are and who we may become (Matus, 2006). Examining the underlying assumptions behind notions of international students in policies is important because it connects to the erasure and neutrality required to produce the Other, as much as in research as in policy. As research informs policymaking they both act as particular moments on a chain producing meaning. They both give impetus to each other.

As research discourses do not differ in important ways from the policy ones, the cultural production of *bodies in motion*, requires a more critical way to tell their narrations of experience. As Sidhu and Dall'Alba (2012) assert,

> while it is entirely valid to highlight the strengths of universities and nation-states in education marketing, it is equally important that we critically examine the embodied subjectivities assembled for those students and read against the complexities they encounter as raced and gendered subjects. (p. 414)

My analyses looks at a range of studies reported in the literature on international students. Much of this literature is located within the discipline of social psychology and cultural communication and it focuses on required conditions for the adequate provision of effective teaching and learning. I will focus on three main discourses of the international student to exercise the ideas of time and space underlying them. These are the discourse of static subjects, the discourse of normalization, and the discourse of students at risk.

I want to emphasize how disembodiment plays an important role when imagining international students. To produce a disembodied subject, time and space need to be imagined in a particular relation to the subject. The subject is produced with no relation to the particularities of time and space. Then, disembodiment is a way to frame the "'naturalness' and unproblematic nature" (Sidhu and D'Alba, 2012) of international students' experiences. To present international students as people who move from one place to another and experience feelings of isolation, and because of that fact, compensatory practices must be necessary is a way to simplify important processes of mobility. To erase the particularities of time and space is a way to avoid complexity. As Merleau-Ponty (1962–1945) explains, "coming to know does not occur despite the constraints of body, but through the access that embodiment provides to our world. It is through embodiment that we can have it all" (cited in Sidhu and Dall'Alba, 2012, p. 416).

As research discussed in this chapter dissociates who international students are from their gendered, raced, classed movements, then attention to the critical processes of knowing is relevant. As Sidhu and Dall'Alba (2012) note, "Embodiment, then, is a condition for knowing; it makes knowing possible" (p. 416). When discussing the situated characteristics of knowledges, what I refer to is that "disembodiment functions as a political technology, foregrounding flows and shifting attention away from embodied experiences of students and their need for situated knowledges" (Sidhu and Dall'Alba, 2012, p. 428).

An important question that orients this chapter is, how do dominant notions of time and space form part of a larger project to produce the Other as lacking and deficient? Before presenting the discourses I will provide a brief description of universities as international institutions that produce discourses about diversity and international bodies. The documents and language presented belong to the higher education institutions where the participants introduced in chapter three completed their degrees.

UNIVERSITIES AS PRODUCERS OF IDENTITIES

In the following pages, I detail some discourses emanated from universities inspired by the ideals of internationalization and diversity, and how they construct ideas about international students. Currently, universities all over the world, in different degrees, express their commitment to internationalization of education and recognize the benefits of recruiting international students, faculty, and the like. But, what is the expression of those commitments to their role as international institutions? I argue that the construction of the "international" dimension within universities has to do more with rhetorical qualities of language than a complex treatment of diversity and international subjectivities. I present discourses and fragments from an institution where international students (introduced in chapter three) pursued their graduate programs. I focus on conceptions of identities and in the ways this university represents international students. The intersections of definitions around diversity, multiculturalism, and the importance of internationalization create a number of tensions as the university seeks to justify and enact its mission as a public research institution.[2]

The institutional presentation of this university when advertising international programs and studies suggests some interesting ideas about the international dimension:

> to meet these challenges [referring to the international context], we have invested in developing international competence. We have added new international faculty lines and increased the number of study abroad opportunities for students. We have developed new research partnerships with colleagues around the world and added new international courses and international degree programs throughout our campus. We are also initiating a new International Living and Learning Community to facilitate interaction between our domestic and international students.

Interestingly, this quote represents a very pragmatic vision of what the international dimension means in the context of the universities in general. Adding courses and people is seen as a major step in the realization of its goal toward internationalization. These ideas push me to think about universities as places promoting a romantic cosmopolitan air in their educational programs more than complicating the representations they are perpetuating through their politics about international dimensions.

Yet a detailed analysis reveals that policy and practice are characterized by limited understandings of the meanings of *diversity*, the purposes of international education, and the role of the universities in the transnational context. The idea of diversity has been used repeatedly in the university's mission as a leading concept in addition to other values, such as excellence, that are particularly relevant to a leading university. Diversity is assumed to be a fundamental condition for creative thinking, spreading of knowledge, developing a more responsible citizen, and more. But one gets the impression that the university's commitment to diversity is largely in terms of numbers of minorities and international students, rather than more qualitative terms.

For instance, throughout the document it is suggested that the

> University is committed to excellence, and its emphasis on diversity is a vital part of that commitment. All work of the University is informed by and enriched by diversity. By sharing our diverse life experiences, perspectives, and expectations, we create an enriched learning environment. Diversity prepares us for deep and innovative thinking because it challenges us to move beyond our automatic assumptions and reactions. Diversity drives creativity.
>
> ...The University prepares future leaders for a multi-cultural nation and world. Students will be better prepared to lead if they are given the opportunities and the range of perspectives from which to question assumptions, both their own and those common in society.
>
> ...Diversity in the University benefits all of society. It produces more creative ideas, draws greater minds and spreads knowledge to a wider audience. It preserves more of our culture and history, and creates a citizenry more likely to engage in the responsibilities of a democracy.

Interestingly, this draws a close connection between excellence and diversity, adding further significance to the idea of recruiting international students. International graduate students are assumed to add diversity to the campus. Officially, diversity is managed and measured only by numbers of international population in academic programs. Then, the University becomes recognized as diverse because of its ability to recruit and retain international students.

Later, the statement maintains that "in a university, the clash of ideas, the testing of assumptions, the enrichment of culture through exposure to many cultures are vital to the missions of teaching, research, and service." I would like to emphasize the idea of *exposure to difference*, which activates very modernistic understanding of diversity. This difference usually has to do with nationalities and cultures. What I argue is that there is always a risk when diversity is the dominant way to think of difference, therefore it is susceptible to being shaped by other strategic interests (e.g., economic or market). This may lead us to the idea that the construction of international is a very complex category because it helps us to question the prevalence of some discourses over others.

One more statement to help illustrate the image of international students provided by the office at the university in charge of international students support (Newsletter from May, 2002):

> ... consider this: you have probably changed tremendously during your stay here in the United States. You have been *exposed* [italics added] to a *new* [italics added] culture, lifestyle, and set of values. You have probably adapted somewhat to the American way of life, and even *incorporated* [italics added] some American values. Your friends and family back home, on the other hand, have not had the occasion to live, work, and study in the United States [this is an assumption]. They probably expect you to be the same person that you were before you left home. They may exhibit only passing interest in your experiences here, and will probably have difficulty relating to the "new" you. In turn, you may feel *frustrated,* [italics added] *rejected,* [italics added] and *out-of-step* [italics added] with your fellow citizens.
>
> What can you do to ease the difficulty to *reverse culture shock?* [italics added] Prepare yourself mentally for the possibility that you will experience this phenomenon. Understand that this is *normal,* [italics added] just as it is normal to experience cultural shock when in a new country. Be patient. It will take some time to *adapt* [italics added] to life back home. Seek out others who have lived abroad. They can more easily understand some of the issues that concern you. Finally, try to remember the strategies that you used to deal with your initial culture shock in the U.S. and *repeat* [italics added] them back home. Soon you will find yourself feeling "at home" once again.

In italicizing specific words from this passage, my intention has been to stress paternalistic and assimilationist perspectives and ideas of fixity when referring to international students. In expressing issues in this way, universities are normalizing communities without anticipating the relevance and consequences of the international communities within campuses. Their discourses maintain the idea of national and foreign, in opposition to domestic and familiar without allowing more alternative rationales when constructing new subjects. Discourses about international students are framed in a language that makes people exist around centered, unified, and single dimensions of the subject/self. To understand identity in such a fixed fashion is problematic and troubling because it makes international students' experiences and lives far too simple. Thus, part of the problem here is how policies and research constitute, perceive, interpret, and present international students to themselves and to others. Simplistic and monolithical perspectives do not offer a sophisticated analysis of the complexities produced by the combination of loyalties and identities lived and thought by international students. As a critical consequence, universities are built upon the perspective of a society within national state frameworks and lose contact with contemporary practices and subjectivities. These unilateral ideas perpetuated by universities, combined with images produced in research, complicate the context for the production of international students.

BUT WHO IS A LEGITIMATE STUDENT, ANYWAYS?

For several years, particularly after September 11, 2001, there has been a vigorous discussion about who the international student *is* and *should be.* There has been an increase in the processes of verification and monitoring for this group of students22ver the years, the definition of international student has changed. Whereas I make a point to use *international* student, most of the texts talk about the *foreign* student. In 1966, the International Institute of Education (IIE) defined an international student as a citizen of a country other than the United States, enrolled in an institution of higher education, who is requiredto return to the home country upon termination of the course of study. This was an administrative definition of an international student. After 1966, the IIE adopted a new definition of international student that included all foreign nationals fully enrolled at recognized institutions of higher learning, regardless of their visa classifications or stated intentions to stay. Beginning in 1974, the definition was changed again to include only nonimmigrant students. The Open Doors report (2002) defines the international student as

> anyone who is enrolled in courses at institutions of higher education who is not a U.S. citizen, an immigrant (permanent resident) or a refugee. These may include holders of F (student) Visas, H (temporary worker/trainee) Visas, J (temporary educational exchange-visitor) Visas, and M (vocational training) Visas. (Open Doors Report, 2002)

Again, the state's bureaucratic definition has been given prominence here ahead of other cultural definitions. Yet, dominant discourses in international education do not consider questions of interculturalism or international understanding.

Not surprisingly the rhetoric before September 11, 2001, tended to look at the promotion of programs for international students in a very positive and pragmatic way. A document emanating from NAFSA (2002) stated: "it was an unquestioned verity of US foreign policy that programs to promote international understanding advanced the national interest. It was almost universally accepted that educating successive generations of world leaders in the United States constituted an indispensable investment in America's international leadership" (p. 2).

After September 11, 2001, these assumptions have been questioned changing the discussion to who the international student should be and what would be the immigration and security restriction laws to ensure the legitimacy of this group of people. The fact that many of the 19 hijackers on September 11, 2001, were purportedly international students encouraged new scrutiny of how international students should be controlled and monitored.

What complicates matters is that international students do not constitute a homogeneous group, nor do they conform to a specific profile. Ann Kuhlman (1992) has said, international students "are a diverse community with different educational, cultural, economic, and political backgrounds, with differing motivations and aspirations" (p. 23). Members of this group have generally family responsibilities, and often have an established career in their home country. The perceived *loss of status* felt by some international students upon arriving on the US campuses is perhaps the principal factor that differentiates them from undergraduate international students. For many this loss of status is unexpected and can make the adjustment process to a new country and educational system more difficult (Kuhlman, 1992, p. 23). Moreover, "individuals from certain nations even expect a special *guest* treatment to reciprocate the same type of treatment they or their former university have extended to US exchange scholars" (Kuhlman, 1992, p. 24). When this is not available, their feelings of marginalization are intensified.

These special concerns produce an interesting debate regarding who the international student should be and how she or he should be constructed within academia. Missing from these debates is a discussion on the critical issue of who the members of this group of non-immigrants are and in what ways the *images* of these people inform policies and research to regulate their stay in United States. I strongly believe that knowing who the international student is and critically naming the assumptions behind discourses on international students will help us build a more conscious critique on how research govern subjects. Of course, practices of regulation have a major impact on how international students think about themselves and how they articulate and work with their subjectivities.

It is this problem that this chapter addresses. I argue that definitions of international students provided by educational institutions as well as research about them are based on cultural and social assumptions about who they are, revealing a unitary and essentializing understanding of space and time. These definitions shape international students' academic lives in many different ways having significant consequences for their educational experience in university settings. It is imperative to look at what universities and official institutions do in terms of forging a new cultural politics of identity that construct discursive languages deeply affecting students' lives. I argue that it is vital to unpack these assumptions because they limit and restrict international students' academic experiences perpetuating asymmetrical and unilateral relations of power in university contexts. To the contrary, I believe that a more complex understanding of space, time, and subjectivity is needed to better reflect the present processes of identity formation within the current context of globalization and the internationalization of US higher education. In these terms, the critical reflections of students' own lived experiences are a potentially powerful tool for articulating new language and new ideas to develop future policies for graduate programs in universities.

FLOWS

While the flow of graduate and undergraduate international students and faculty across borders has extensive historical precedents, the characteristics of the present flow of international movement of this community differ from those of the past. One of the main differences is that the numbers involved are much larger today than was the case in previous years, but perhaps the most important distinction between the travel practices of the present from those in the past is that today the general pattern of international flow is being described as unidirectional. Despite minor variations, the stability in the general flow since World War II is clear and is related to the overall trend of students to go from countries of the periphery to the countries at the center. Even though it is no longer adequate to map the globe into binary zones of center and periphery, I think it is important to illustrate the dynamics of these movements for future discussion (see Wilson and Dissanayake, 1996; Lulat and Altbach, 1985). Lulat and Altbach (1985) have said that the patterns in the transnational migration of students show that Third World nations look to the industrialized nations as models of how to *modernize* their own countries. By studying abroad, students not only learn Western technical skills but also cultural styles, norms, and values of the West. However, Fazal Rizvi (2000) demonstrates that this idea of uncontrolled Westernization is misplaced. He claims that while it is true, "the movement of students for education is largely unidirectional, but this does not imply that the international students soak up every cultural message they encounter in the West" (p. 221). What it is interesting in here is how the way of organizing the world as center and periphery produces a "range of connections between the imagination of the spatial and the imagination of the political" (Massey, 2005, p. 10). In other words, the way to think about the flows of international students and the privileging of the western orientation of their education is an integral part in the constitution of who they are as outsiders, including the political aspects of their location: their *home countries* become a reference for their politics.

THE DISCOURSE OF STATIC SUBJECTS

The persistent uses of the polarization of the world perpetuate the power relation between the binaries and create the contours from which to live the experience of being an outsider. What matters here is how research studies maintain this notion of supremacy and intellectual colonization, where the international student is portrayed as a subject who *acquires* knowledge from a specific culture and mobilizes it in her/his own country. For instance, most of the studies provide information on how to be successful in US classrooms following research-based principles, presenting correlations between language proficiency, learning strategies, academic success, and so on (Abela, 2002). How these practices install ideas in the imagination of institutions and people is important. Dominant notions of space and time have abiding influences on the ways these conclusions are created. The linear understanding of processes presented in these research studies and the ways of imagining space as neutral are critical ways to theorize about the constitution of subjects. As Doreen Massey (2005) sustains, space is produced in the negotiation of relations where the social is constructed. As the US education is presented as significantly different and superior to education in other countries, other nations will be imagined undoubtedly as inferior, lacking, and behind.

The common belief that international students *learn* values and norms also presents a concern. This emphasis on *learning* the values of the Western academic culture signals a unidirectional way to relate to the world. This imagination of the Other approaching another territory with its own restricted set of attributes overlooks imaginations of time and space to read these assumptions as natural.

What research studies do is to reproduce the popular idea that international students belong to a homogeneous group, to a specific territory and culture. In so doing, research shapes a cultural and social context making international students a target of damaging definitions and labels often expressed in terms of deficits. In this sense research studies and policies have the power to inscribe in people's mind and bodies a specific system ruling their actions. Within this context, research studies help to create the data and arguments to justify ways to organize and regulate international students' subjectivities, desires, and imagination.

Another interesting idea is to explore on how universities can "improve their chances of retaining international students by providing students with help in adjusting to the U.S. higher education" (Lacina, 2002, p. 25). For instance, "crisis situations may develop for the international student as a result of the transition to a new culture and social environment" (Sakurako, 2000, pp. 140). What interests me here is the notion of the *new*. How the unknown takes the status of new is important within the linear rhetoric of progress. To believe the new is ahead implies that the (real) past plays a significant role in constructing the present. To recognize an experience as new implies that my previous experiences take the status of left behind. The future then becomes the promise of the accumulation of past experiences. This sounds logical, right? My concern relates to the ways in which theorizing about space and time and their integral relationship allows us to speak about multiplicity and openness as new configurations that may set off new social processes. As Elizabeth Grosz (1999) proposes, "to rethink temporality in terms of the surprise of the new, the inherent capacity for time to link, in extraordinarily complex ways, the past and present to a future that is uncontained by them and has the capacity to rewrite and transform them" (p. 7).

Other ways to speak of international students in research studies emphasize that "overall, international students' experience more problems in college than American students do. However, studies suggest that even though many international students are very much in need of psychological help, mental health services are generally underused by these students" (Lacina, 2002, p. 22). As presented in these kinds of studies, the idea of the static subject is characterized as an identity, in terms of "mutual recognition, as if one's identity depended on the recognition by others" (Kellner, 1992, 233). The idea that only international students under the stress of the completion of a degree suffer more than US students legitimates and makes the experience of international students trustable and predictable. They come to occupy a recognizable position. In these terms, identity is circumscribed to a set of attributes and dispositions: one is a *nonimmigrant*, a *student*, a *foreigner*, and the like or rather a combination of these social roles and positions. Identities are viewed as restricted, fixed, and limited, within the boundaries of the possible identities provided by particular discourses (Kellner, 1992). However, in different ways many of the hegemonic discourses produced in research about international students do sustain themselves by the assumptions that space is instant, divided, and produces a specific tempo for this community. In other words, I want to pose the question to the ways that ideas of time and space organize and perpetuate inequalities.

In a different group of studies the issues of language barriers, social competences, problem solving, social adjustment, political, financial, and organizational dimension of studying abroad are analyzed. For instance, Lulat and Altbach (1985, p. 456) propose that one of the main problems for international students is that of readjustment to the home country. Once back in their local environments, a factor that has been reported as problematic for international students is their inability to work effectively, mainly because the working conditions are inadequate or drastically different. Besides the totalizing quality of this thinking, I would argue that coming back to their own countries makes international students vulnerable because their subjectivities have been displaced and destabilized, consequently fragmenting their imaginations of social and cultural realities. And this phenomenon is produced not because international students *have lived in a different country,* but because of the more complicated processes of dealing and confronting the meanings of being subjected to limited notions of who they are and where they come from.

The assumptions are discussed to highlight a common experience of time, a universal time where spatialized ideas of productivity and competences can be realized.

THE DISCOURSE OF NORMALIZATION

In another study, Andrea Trice (2000) analyzes the perceptions of faculty toward international students. She stresses the lack of and need for research on how to work with international students understanding that they are different from their U.S.' counterparts. Faculty interviewed for her study expressed that "they had become more adept at working with international students through trial and error only" (p. 30). This element not only draws attention to the lack of understanding on who the international student is but also, more importantly, suggests how international students are produced in discourse as *objects* to be normalized by the curriculum and policies. What is relevant is the range of *problems* identified by faculty. For instance, participants noted a "marked segregation of domestic and international students caused in part by language barriers" (Trice, 2000, p. 35). Language, as an important sign for the production of a deficient Other, plays an important role. As is, the international student is created in difference and exclusion, where she/he is seen as the *Other* within the structure of prevailing power relations. Most faculty in this literature recognize English as a major hurdle for these students, which constitutes the most visible element upon which to lay the blame when discussing international students' *problematic* experiences. Language as representing a cultural production of the subject imposes a specific identity to those thought as outsiders. Language relates to deficit and limited possibilities. In some ways, issues of social class come to the fore when analyzing these pieces of research. Proficiency in English as a second language connects to the ideas of "cultural capital" as vital to construct hierarchies among those who have the experiences of international students in the United States.

As I discuss different images of the international student, what is clear is the prevalence of modernistic ideas of time, space, and subjectivity. Besides the existing defined and available roles, norms, and expectations for international students, producing knowledge about international students in this way is a complex process of exclusion and misrepresentation. As Kellner (1992) notes, "the Other is a constituent of identity in modernity and, consequently, the Other—directed character is a familiar type in late modernity, dependent upon others for recognition and thus for the establishment of personal identity" (p. 142). An important point put forward by Stuart Hall (1996) that can be helpful in talking about this notion of the Other, is that identities, are the positions which the subject is obliged to take up while always "knowing" that they are representations, that representation is always constructed across the "lack," across a division, from the place of the Other, and thus can never be adequate—identical—to the subject processes which are invested in them. (p. 6)

To understand identity this way is to close up or limit the possibility of the unconventional. There is no recognized space for the untidy narratives that destabilize the conventional forward motion of narratives of international movement.

Most studies on international students assume that international movement is rooted in the relation of people coming from less-developed countries to people from developed countries. As this imaginary is sustained by an essentialist view of identity that assures that the identity shared by members of a social group will remain stable and based on collective, self-evidently meaningful experience of space and time. To normalize international students' experiences in research in a substantive way is to risk reproducing lack of movement thereby distorting the multiple and tricky meanings lived because of movement.

The idea of the normal identity of the international student implies a way to occupy space and a way to experience time. As international students, "entering" a space already containing "its corresponding identities" they become the suspect, the unknown, the stranger. As the supremacy of territory is produced through whiteness, conventional masculinity, the abled body, the international student will come from a place, another territory that is located back in line. To sustain that international students belong to a territory and that they exhibit *the* culture of that place implies that we are using a language that holds captive dominant understandings of time, space, and subjectivity.

THE DISCOURSE OF STUDENTS AT RISK

For over thirty years, scholars in the field of intercultural communication have produced extensive research on *behavior patterns* of international students when studying abroad (see Gudykunst, 1998; 2003). My assertion is that trying to group international students under the same *behavioral patterns* is a strategy to maintain clear and well-delimited groups. Rather, these studies essentialize international students' identities by not paying attention to the complexities and interpretations of their selves within the university setting. Noemi Marin (1996) proposes that pressures due to time limitations and to a high level of performance required from the very beginning put international graduate students in a disadvantageous position as they have to produce high-quality work while dealing with cultural, social, and linguistic differences between themselves and US graduate students. In this study, notions that hegemonic time operates as universal are important to pay attention to.[3] As Sarah Sharma (2014) notes, "There is a cultural expectation that people must do their best at all times to fit within the temporal order" (p. 145). In examining the difficulties for graduate students in adapting to the different expectations that graduate school places upon them, Marin (1996) states that international students are students *at risk* because they become central foci for cultural tensions in relation to educational values, sociocultural and linguistic norms appropriate to graduate programs of study. What is relevant here for my analysis is the fact that international students live within borders of cultural tensions derived from the very dominant notions of time and space that produce and maintain international students' positions. In other words, rules of socialization in a graduate program reflect cultural practices in which international graduate students see themselves as the Other. The production of "the student at risk" is based on the valuation of attributes that can be seen as required to perform in institutions. In this case, issues of gender, sexuality, race, and social class play an important role for the valuation of identities and practices. The production of the student at risk works in such a way that it fosters a notion of the normal student with certain attributes. As mentioned earlier some characteristics such as English proficiency, ways to cope with the *new culture,* are ways to value particular cultural and social practices. The association of experiences of international movement with the notion of risk is confined to discourses of class, gender, race, etc. It appears that the production of international students in policies, university documents, and popular institutional discourse is not complete without the idea that in some ways this population is at risk. Research studies presenting variables that may affect the experiences of this group of people inform, and in turn are informed by, expert knowledge relating to communication, social, and psychological disciplines.

As indicated already, I do not question the fragility of the experiences of international students and the profound alienation and discrimination they may go through. However, I am disturbed by the continuous reproduction of the "common knowledge" that the experience of international movement and to live in a place different from your own effectively increases people's social and cultural problems. The legitimate truths underlying these ways to talk about international students are based on specific ways to think and talk about space and time.[4] As Mary Lou Rasmussen (2004) proposes, "When expert knowledges are construed as political practices linked to relations of power, it is apparent that what passes for normal is, and will always be, contested" (p. 135). Certainly, the relation between "risk" and international students is of interest.

MOVING THOUGHTS

All of the discourses I have discussed above create hierarchies of oppression rather than acknowledging the complex interdependencies between space, time, and subjectivities. As these discourses emphasize the definition of the subject from an essentialist point of view, particular aspects of identity are presented as the sole cause of determinant social meanings of individual experiences. As discourses of the static subject, normalization, and student at risk coexist alongside with discourses of excellence and exceptionalism, the contradictions presented in the field of internationalization of higher education are evident.

Most research studies about international students portray the international student's experience as problematic and as part of an assimilation process, giving little room for the recognition of the intersectional dynamics between movement, culture, race, gender, class, nationality, and so on. My aim in this chapter has been to show that studies about international students' experiences are framed in a language that does not open up spaces for questioning or revitalize the conversations about multiple aspects of space, time, and subjectivity. On the contrary, I think these studies position the international student in a space where they are considered problematic and where the discourses about them become the norm governing and demarcating the students' lives. In these studies, the constructs of identity and the international student have been discussed in a very static way. As such, there have been many spaces and intersections, which have not been explored. Moreover, presenting international students as students being *at risk*, anticipating *behavioral patterns*, presenting language as a *barrier*, and the like, promotes the imposition of labels on these students, permanently positioning them in an isolated, atypical remote place. In contrast, I think the concern would be more appropriately placed on the improvization of identities rather than one unified identity. I think it is vital to move the discussion on international students to a different place where different concepts of time and space can be used in order to illuminate people's experiences. The emergence of a new language to expand the conversation on international students and their movement is critical when talking about processes in higher education in the global context.

The general aim of this chapter has been to recognize the effects of research discourses about international students and show how they imprint a position to be lived by subjects. Once the subject has been positioned, this individual is expected to and is likely to see, live, and imagine the world from this place. In this way, policies and research discourses limit and impede alternative possibilities of imagining the subjects' lives, dreams, and aspirations. I have shown how the often taken-for-granted assumptions about international students have the power to reinforce negative constructions of who they are. This often distorts the worlds inhabited by these students.

In the context of universities as sites of strict regulation of international students, knowledge creates their experiences as lacking and deviant. Specific ideas of time and space operate behind these naturalizations. Internationalization practices in universities operate as normalizing of time and space. These practices prescribe in many different ways how time and space should be lived.

As universities propose a singular and universal understanding of experience, as presented in chapter two, international students tell their stories of positioning in relation to those trajectories of authenticity and unchanging identities. Universities, as space exist prior to those identities given to international students. In here, the importance "of the spatiality of the production of knowledge itself" (Massey, 2005, p. 63) is crucial to question the production of categories and differentiations between international students and domestic students. What universities do is to create experiences in complete predictability for international students. As the matrix of space and time is recognizable, experiences are told as the container of past, present, and future possibilities. And, as space is understood as a prior entity, international students' ways to narrate are predictable in that they claim for spaces and times given to them. Spatial and temporal categories, the home, the inside, the outside, the past, the future, all play an important role when describing lived experiences. The assumption that "time is a line with a beginning and end, running through or alongside space" (Massumi, 2002, p. 202) is crucial to understand the practices and discourses of international students' experiences.

CHAPTER 5

LANDSCAPES OF THE BODY: DESIRING SPACE OTHERWISE

...and in a month or so I'll sometimes fall asleep with the sound of whales moving about in the bay, they blow through their air holes, and breath in the cool night air, and soon I'm hoping for an iceberg to drift by. We usually get a few passing by, some have come in on the wind and got stuck on the bottom of the bay...The bay is very deep...I'm blessed to have such a place...I don't know of another place to anchor myself but next to an ocean. The light can be very moving (Email from a participant, May, 2006).

In this chapter, I trouble the "path" that defines who we are in relation to places. I explore how the imaginations of place define what bodies might become. I look at how taken-for-granted understandings of place, as a container ready to be filled in, act upon us to normalize and anticipate positions for ourselves and others. This understanding of space as occupied by things, identities, meanings, and practices (Massey, 2005) confines the self as someone we already know. To orient oneself to space in predefined ways or to inhabit spaces as already oriented (Ahmed, 2006) reproduces social and cultural imaginations. In this respect, Doreen Massey (2005) comments, "So easily this way of imagining space can lead us to conceive of other places, peoples, cultures simply as phenomena 'on' this surface...They lie there, on space, in place, without their own trajectories" (p. 4).

In this chapter, I work with narratives of the international students introduced in chapter 3 to understand how orientations toward spaces define how we inhabit those spaces. It is my contention that international students' notions of who they are, are intrinsically related to ideas of place. For instance, much of their narratives signal spatial ideas to refer to their experiences of arriving, returning, imaginaries of the home country, the host country, narrations of origin and departure, all of them indicating starting and ending positions. Discourses that emanate from institutional policies and research studies that describe international students' experiences, frequently speak to a naturalization of particular experiences within implicit spatial frames of reference, such as nation, race, social class, sexuality, and so on. In this chapter, these naturalizing discourses are critical because spatial imaginaries demand constant construction and reproduction of the taken-for-granted meanings attached to places that, in turn, reinforce a chain of essentialized discourses.

I intend to question "the path" that defines who international students are in relation to places, and by doing this, explore how this way of "following" how the already established representations and meanings attached to those places normalizes ideas of bodies inhabiting those places. As Sarah Ahmed (2006) contends, "We follow the line that is followed by others: the repetition of the act of following makes the line disappear from view as the point from which 'we' emerge" (p. 15). Therefore, much of this argument is about what we might become if we abandon, even for a moment, pre-existing and inevitable notions of place, and pay attention to more provocative conceptualizations for understanding our relations to places, including movement, continuous variation, transitions, events, and durational space (Massumi, 2002).

This chapter explores how international students orient themselves to established imaginations of places. As Ahmed (2006) explains, "If space is always orientated, as Lefebvre argues, then inhabiting spaces 'decides' what comes into view" (p. 14). Place, understood as "an empty receptacle, independent of its contents" (Grosz, 1995, p. 92) normalizes ideas of the self and the relations between the subject and the objects, meanings, symbols, and practices *occupying* that place. This conceptualization of place suggests the anticipation of acts of becoming, the creation of meanings, and the reproduction of truths about the world we live in.

The current global context, characterized by the continuous mobility of various communities, flows of information and images, demands attention to the ways subjects are imagined. The ways to imagine subjects' positions are not defined as action (Grosz, 1999), but as a *re*action to preexisting categories. Positioning subjects as action undermines the static conceptualizations of place as a useful theoretical tool to refer to the meanings of experiences of people moving around the world. It is my contention that discourses that imagine place as a container perpetuate ideas of the subject occupying locations. The formation of international students' identity or theories of cultural deficiency that label international students as "students at risk," as presented in chapter four, repeat associations of subjects with already established notions of place (Calhoun, 2003; Clifford, 1989).

This way to imagine the subject occupying positions on a pre-given structure reproduces a series of oppositional cultural constructions, that are in need of interruption (for example, First World/Third World, rich/poor countries, developed economies/transitional economies, white/black, gay/straight, etc.) (Massumi, 2002). This traditional conceptualization of place constructs the body as the configuration (Massumi, 2002) of preestablished characteristics located on a congruent and readable pattern. To think and perform places as containers of experiences, identities, symbols, signs, and practices requires the imagination of the self as being confined to someone we already know, a predefined self (who is very different from the body itself) (Grosz, 1999) who *fits* the predetermined matrix. This notion of place requires the constant confirmation of affinities between the self and the already-made spatial categories (nation, margin, center, outside, international, Third World, etc.). The oppositional frameworks produced by the idea of subjects occupying space, work as a grid where subjects locate themselves and, at the same time, work actively to establish a correspondence between the subject and the "site" (Massumi, 2002). As Massumi (2002) reminds us about the purpose of the works on positionality,

> Of course, a body occupying one position on the grid might succeed in making a move to occupy another position. In fact certain

normative progressions, such as that from child to adult, are coded in. But this doesn't change the fact that what defines the body is not the movement itself, only its beginnings and endpoints. (p. 3)

The imaginaries of spaces as points in time, and the assigned role of bodies inhabiting them is a way to essentialize and reproduce cultural frameworks. I believe that paying attention to movement[1] and questioning the reproduction of ideas that conceive place as surface can help us interrupt dominant cultural frameworks that constrain our experiences of movement. It is my contention that the ways international students narrate their own trajectories are more focused on ideas of space as a surface with less attention on their experiences of movement.[2] What we usually recount about their experiences are cultural snapshots. We zoom in and zoom out from places to give accounts of people's experiences in relation to those places. We follow "paths" to narrate stories of movement relying on static notions of place.

The interviews I will present in this chapter are part of a study with international students in the United States between 2001 and 2003. In this research, I focused on the constructions of narratives of (de) orientation when international students speak about their stories of travel and the meanings of inhabiting places. In many ways, their stories spoke to me about the complexities and unveiled aspects of their experiences and how their senses of "being in motion" could offer a possibility to rethink meanings of places. In the work I did with international students they revealed the frequently conflicting values assigned to places, geographies, and subjects related to those places.

An important dimension of their journey that frame their experiences in the United States are the immigration regulations that control different aspects of their stay, such as the amount of time they have to finish their graduate degrees, periodicity of travelling abroad, reporting address changes, among others. These are discussed in chapters three and four.

When analyzing the interviews I look for meanings and discourses that talk about the relations between places and the construction of the experiences of these international students. In order to orient my analysis I work with these three questions: What do ideas of places as surfaces do to the ways international students inhabit and imagine places? What are the uses of preconfigured identities given to international students in relation to places? And how do subjects narrate a way out of the preestablished ways to imagine places?

In this chapter, I provide a synopsis of three main concepts for the analysis: space/place, orientation, and movement. I believe that going deeper into the ways these three concepts help us understand the ways we relate to places is critical. To problematize the correspondence between the subject and place inhabited is political in that it provides specific cultural and social positions to occupy.

UNDERSTANDING SPACE/PLACE, MOVEMENT, AND ORIENTATION

One way to enter into the discussion on how we speak and live with dominant spatialities in mind is to refer to the distinction between space and place. The usual representation of space and place is as two separate entities. Place expresses a more concrete way to imagine spatial entities while space refers more to the abstract.[3] It is through the imagination of space and place that we have come to believe that the concrete (place) is more real than the abstract (space) (Massey, 2005). In this respect, Doreen Massey (2005) reminds us, "One cannot seriously posit space as the outside of place as lived, or simply equate 'the everyday' with the local. If we really think space relationally, then it is the sum of all our connections, and in that sense utterly grounded, and those connections may go round the world" (p. 185). The implications of imagining space and place, as distinctive dimensions of how we *are* in the world, is a product of dominant ways to imagine the relation of the self and rhetorics of space. In Doreen Massey's (2005) words, "[the]argument is not that place is not concrete, grounded, real, lived, etc. It is that space is too" (p. 185).

For the purposes of this chapter, place is no longer seen as the surface containing objects, subjects and meanings, and space is not the inevitable "out there." Imagining space and place in this way, the self is assumed to be recognizable, intelligible, someone we already know. To build experiences following the imagination of space as a container suggests to "build in predictability" (Massumi, 2002,

p. 204). Questioning this orientation in our thinking about space and place has implications for the constitution of subjects inhabiting those spaces.

In this chapter, place is conceptualized as created out of social relations (Massey, 1994), and as such, they are embedded in relations of power. Place as the effect of social relations resignifies boundaries among places and makes spaces recognizable entities. The lines that maintain spaces intact make us "find," "construct," and "create" a place. In other words, I have to move and imagine I am getting to somewhere. That somewhere, is understood as always uncertain, a possibility, a fragile construction. It may be read as *action* and *force* that make possible the transformation of ideas of places, subjects, and their relations. For me, place as the force coming out of the ways we relate to the world, opens the possibility to narrate the self off the path. To inhabit a place means to construct "the self" as the one who narrates. This poses place as a possibility of becoming, a possibility to imagine the subject's way out of definitional and preconfigured culturally and socially congruent structures.

I hope at this point that the ideas of space presented by Deleuze and Guattari (1987) are of help. They talk about space as striated and smooth where the first one "...organizes even the desert; [and] in the second, the desert grains and grows, and the two happen simultaneously" (p. 474). The possibilities offered by these two representations to understand space might be better captured by the image of dots and lines. In a striated space, lines and dots are arranged to follow an organized and predictable order. The lines connect the dots. Lines are possible only in relation to the dot. In a smooth space there is no order to follow and lines and dots represent a chaotic arrangement of directions, variations, pauses, and pulses. As Deleuze and Guattari (1987) explain, "In striated space, lines or trajectories tend to be subordinated to points: one goes from one point to another. In the smooth, it is the opposite: the points are subordinated to the trajectory" (p. 478). Through describing international students' intrinsic relation to spaces and movement in light of these ideas, I argue that the narration of their experiences of movement and meanings of inhabiting places depends on how they imagine spaces. In other words, whether the smooth or striated prevails in the imagination of space.

To imagine oneself as more related to the striated space (though we are always on both) implies the subjection of the body occupying a position on the pregiven structure. As Massumi (2002) explains, "the idea of positionality begins by substracting movement from the picture. This catches the body in cultural freeze-frame. When positionality of any kind comes a determining first, movement comes a problematic second" (p. 3). The ways we "follow" preestablished ideas of inhabiting places perpetuate the coherence and correspondence between places and those bodies inhabiting them.

In opposition to this passive understanding of place Claire Colebrook (1996), signaling Foucault's archaeology of the human sciences, notes that, "the subject [is] an effect of a certain type of question" (p. 122). In the case international students' experiences of inhabiting places, the common questions to which they have to be confronted express the passivity with which spaces are imagined. Many of the questions that relate to international students' experiences speak of places as points of origins or arrival: Where do you come from? What is your country of origin?, and so on. These questions reinforce the coincidence between the subject and the place of reference. In other words, these questions secure the coincidence with an already-established idea of who she/he is and where she/he comes from. So what would be the question that reflects more the idea of variation or movement? As Massumi (2002) states, "when a body is in motion, it does not coincide with itself. It coincides with its own transition: its own variation" (p.4).

As my interest is focused on *bodies in motion,* movement becomes a relevant concept to explore. To read international students' and academics' experiences of movement as static, as defined by the departure or end points is a way to subtract the very definition of what they are experiencing. As some theorists state (Massumi, 2002; Manning, 2003) the opposite to movement is positionality, which means that we read and locate subjects' experiences, practices, identities within a cultural grid that structures the ways we are perceived by others and by themselves. As Massumi (2002) explains,

...a body occupying one position on the grid might succeed in making a move to occupy another position. In fact, certain normative progressions, such as that from child to adult, are coded in. But this doesn't change the fact that what defines the body is not the movement itself, only its beginnings and endpoints. Movement is entirely subordinated to the positions it connects. These are pre-defined. (p. 3)

What is important here is to explore in the transformative attribute of movement itself. As I have been showing in different chapters of this book, the narration of different trajectories of movement tell about the transformation of ways to understand home, identity, fear, nation, and so on. These are narratives that show the qualitative transformation in those discourses that inform movement. To believe that academic *bodies in motion,* only document stories of displacement and attachment has political effects for rethinking higher education institutions. It is a way to maintain ideas of the unity of the subject who leaps from one place to another, and ideas of space as containing bodies and practices that are clearly divisible. And time is maintained as the explanation for advancement, progress, and deficit. As if everything is already set up. This has important implications for the production of the politics of institutional spaces. They organize its practices around notions of movement as leaping from one place to another, but pay little attention to the transformations that affect, for instance, the meanings of knowledge and research. Then, to imagine that academics moving around the world leaping from one territory to another is a way to simplify the complexities of movement itself. The image of academics leaping is to erase movement from the story (Massumi, 2002). As I show in different chapters and by using different narratives, *bodies in motion* are understood through questions of what it is and where it is. It is through multiple national and local regulations, through cultural hierarchies, that academics respond to. To allow the production of their experiences of movement through the tellings of their transitions from one point to another, to document their frustrations and accomplishments while in another territory, to mobilize knowledge to their home countries, all these imaginaries erase the quality of movement itself when delimiting the story to tell. Then, movement as related to space and orientation is the way *bodies in motion* may complicate their tellings of what it is, what it does, and what it means to move.

The concept of orientation, meaning how we "reside in space" (Ahmed, 2006, p. 1), is important for this analysis. Orientation represents the different "path" we take to capture a space. If space is understood as a surface to be occupied, then spaces act on us as limitations, as already-given meanings to be inhabited. Spaces in this case, represent how "bodies take shape" (Ahmed, 2006, p. 2). And this is particularly important when studying the performativity of the alignment between places and bodies inhabiting those places. As Sarah Ahmed (2006) explains, "Orientations shape not only how we inhabit space, but how we apprehend this world of shared inhabitance, as well as "who" or "what" we direct our energy and attention toward" (p. 3). These orientations direct international students to recognize the "same object" (Ahmed, 2006, p. 118). For instance, a student from Kenya living in the US Midwest is required to recognize objects, directions, intensities in relation to who he is and the meanings of "acquiring" this space. As Ahmed (2006) explains, "space then becomes a question of 'turning,' of direction taken, which not only allow things to appear, but also enable us to find our way through the world by situating ourselves in relation to such things" (p. 6).

International students use imaginaries of places to inhabit them, therefore, subject themselves to already-established relations between place and subjects, meanings and practices occupying those places.

PLACING IDENTITIES. ZOOMING OUT/IN SPACES

Now I turn to troubling the relation between international students' "identities" and the places through which these identities are both produced and expressed. I believe that the critical reproduction of the correspondence of subjects and places experienced by international students, has to do with traditional uses of imaginations of space and place, and how these imaginaries align bodies to spaces. The problematic relations between places and preconceived ideas of the subject shape the boundaries of space, affecting the meanings of "being" in that space.

If narratives of movement are able to interrupt ideas of attachment, then to question those strict affiliations to races, cultures, languages, or backgrounds imposed on international students represents a critical approach to how we understand the relation between identity and place (Massey, 1994).[4] So, what do narratives of movement provoke about the ways spatial categories are imagined? International students' experiences of movement are stories of orientations and disorientations in relation to places. The starting points from where they refer to themselves, as "from where the world unfolds," (Ahmed, 2006, p. 8) happen on simultaneous levels, cultures, continents, places, languages, and epistemologies. Their experiences are full of contradictions and questionings about fixed concepts that traditionally give stability to life, such as home (McDowell, 1999). For instance, when asked for notions of home, one of the interviewees answers:

> Home clearly means different things. Now, I see it differently. So, I don't know, it is difficult because when you say *home* this is what I think. When I was in Nairobi, home always referred to my rural origins, the place I come from, which is about 400 miles, 300 miles from Nairobi into the rural areas of western Kenya. Nairobi itself did not figure as home. Now, when I came here [the U.S.], the immediate thought of home was the whole of that Kenya. So all of that Kenya is my home. But now, after living here for some time, I realize that home is also the place where I reside here. So, at this point it becomes difficult for me to answer a question such as what is, where is your home? Or where do you come from? Because it becomes, like, normal whether to think Chicago or Washington, or to say Kenya, or whether to say western Kenya, which is my rural home. So, home is really a multiple word, word with multiple meanings to me at least.

This quote helps us understand the ways that imaginaries about space perpetuate the idea of "the subject as a point in space, and not the focal point around which an ordered space is organized" (Grosz, 1995, p. 90). The ways he speaks of his relation to space can be represented by the idea of boxes inside boxes, the idea of zooming out or in spaces. One "starts" somewhere to "arrive" somewhere else. This recreated sense of attachment is understood as an impulse to interpret oneself in the moving construction of who we are in relation to different rhetorics of space.

Home, belonging, and detachment are the expressions of the modern relation between time and space. Home in here is used as a discourse of security, of national coherence to a community that is excluded. Home is a discourse of "national identity" and racialization. As Erin Manning (2003) explains

> With "identity" as the necessary presupposition, the frame is simply set on its side; thus, for instance, a surface reading might suggest that the racialization of culture is no longer what is at stake, even while this very racialization continues to prevent a critical renegotiation of the subject-position within the discourse of the nation-state. (p. 61)

As a result, the ways to produce the idea of the international student is framed under a depoliticized notion of identity itself, which sets the conversations on issues of racism, sexism, and the like to a reaction toward the Other. If we critically seek to reposition ourselves within the discourse of identity

> we must realize that any reading of identity is always also a rereading of the possibility of identity itself. Identity as a reconceptualization of the limits of the national imaginary must always be that which under construction, refigured and disfigured by the other. For such a deconstruction of identity to take place, the other must no longer be the accessible and identifiable measure of difference negotiated by the powerful center. Encounters must be challenging, and, as such, they must subvert the boundary formations that seek to prevent a traversal and translation of texts. (Manning, 2003, p. 62)

In this case, research conclusions act as mechanisms that guarantee the preservation of essentialized ideas of culture and identity. Research studies on international students are based on historical notions of the Other and represent a linear and hierarchical relation with the Other that relies on a specific organization of time and space as presented in chapter 4. When research presents international students as lacking, in deficit what they are saying is that there is a "natural" way of thinking of progress and advancement. For instance, when Erin Manning (2003) discusses the role of historiography in the production of nation ness she states,

> History "progresses" by selecting and defining this "other," basing its mastery of expression upon what the other keeps silent, either because the other is not "there" to respond or because the other has not been given the tools to speak. Historiography thus uses the past to articulate a law that inscribes (national) identity and unity, discarding any narrative remains that counter the homogeneity of the nation as bounded community. Rather than describing the silent practices that construct it, historiography effects a new distribution of already semanticized practices. (p. 63)

In this case, I am interested in understanding how the university acts as a text where the guest and the host inhabit the same structure. Research, then, acts as a nationalizing feature of both, the host and the guest, it works as a mechanism to reinstall the limits of times and spaces of the Other.

UNEASY TERRITORIES

In this section, I will show how the participant from Kenya narrates and gives us some insights on how attachment to territories plays an important aspect of the retelling of the experience of movement and the construction of places to inhabit. In one of our conversations he talked about how weather conditions shape his stay in the United States and help him define himself: "...I didn't grow up in extreme weather conditions. The winter and the summer have been quite hard. The summer is too hot. It's uncomfortable for me. The winter is too cold. It's uncomfortable for me because in my country temperatures are between 60° and 80° throughout the year." The notion of being attached to landscapes as new senses of belonging is also presented in other interactions I had with participants:

> ...the trouble is that it has been my experience that feelings of dissonance or displacement never leave. I feel like an outsider most of the time. Here in southern Canada I'm able to find my way. I can escape

deep into the woods or climb down a cliff and watch the play of light
on a reef or headland. The land and sea keep me balanced.

　... maybe because we need to understand ourselves so radically profound that we need the "other" to interpret ourselves
through... The "other," most of the time, it is an inanimate/inti-
mate other.... nature, water, breeze, fog... beauty... light.... but
I think, at some point, we feel the discomfort in our bodies... and
then we start looking for some more careful talking.... then it gets
mixed up with fears... and we run away.... Now... I accept the
running away... as part of me... writing my own page... not as
something I need to change.... You know.... sometimes I think it
is time to trust.

To orient oneself to landscapes and senses of weather is another
expression of international students' "finding their way" or "feeling at home" (Ahmed, 2006, p. 9). The ways the participant
describes his connections to experiencing weather is another way
to describe what it means to align the body with spaces. In other
words, weather acts as a "homing device" (Ahmed, 2006, p. 9).
Sarah Ahmed (2006) explains, "In a way, we learn what home
means, or how we occupy space at home and as home, when we
leave home" (p. 9). This description of being attached to landscapes and senses of weather is another way to orient the subject
to the self "in" here. Home, as the temporary construction of the
self in relation to a place, reminds us that spaces are not far away
from our bodies (Ahmed, 2006). To conceive of space through
orientation means that we follow already designed and preestablished meanings that occupy and constitute that space. Spaces,
then, acquire directions, and "homes are effects of the histories of
arrival" (Ahmed, 2006, p. 9). These are the ways in which international students interpret and narrate the meanings of home as
part of their trajectories.[5]

NARROW CORRESPONDENCES

Now I turn to troubling the ways international students' narratives
reproduce correspondences between places and subjectivities. I contend that experiences of racism, xenophobia, among others, lived by

international students, depend on traditional ideas of space and place held by the collective imagination.

As I mentioned earlier, the participants of this study, like many of the graduate international students who come to the United States, have extensive academic trajectories in their home countries. However, in order to come to the United States, they are required to prove legitimacy through complex policies and regulations. Moreover, contemporary US notions of "terrorism" have targeted international students as subjects of suspicion, which problematizes even more the imagination of the international student's "identity." And as previously mentioned, the absoluteness of spatial categories in which international students are constructed is almost never questioned. Current policies and regulations about international students, often refuse to acknowledge students' fragmented and multiple experiences. Rather, policies and regulations continue to force the alignment between the subject and the taken-for-granted cultural, social, and political positions attributed to their "countries of origin." To better represent the complexity of the relations between places and subjectivities Massey (1994) proposes that, "the identity of a place does not derive from some internalized history. It derives, in large part, precisely from the specificity of its interactions with 'the outside'" (p. 169). In other words, international students constructed as suspicious subjects signals specific ways to construct relations between the United States and the rest of the world. September 11's discourses of threat facilitated the emergence of a new dimension of the category of "international student" where the status of a dangerous outsider was consolidated (Matus, 2006).

To imagine the world, and who you and others are on it, under the assumption that we occupy positions in a predefined cultural structure, produces contradictory statements such as the ones presented by the participant from Kenya when talking about how he is perceived in the United States:

> I have been identified as a poor person who is likely to get involved in crime, such as stealing [in the U.S.]. I have been seen with suspicion in that perspective. Once you tell someone you come from Africa, they

begin to ask a lot about diseases, about hunger and so many things like that. They also see you as suffering from all these diseases. The worst has been at the University Clinic. Anytime I mentioned that I had just arrived from Africa I would be persuaded to take so many tests, medical examinations, including HIV. So the identity I am trying to negotiate here, which has been attached to me is that of a sick person, from a sick nation.

The adjectives used in this paragraph by the international student from Kenya shows how each of these terms, sick, hungry, poor, and criminal, come loaded with particular spatial orientations rooted in the idea that subjectivities correspond to certain imagined places. This is a way to align the body with space, or to "follow" an orientation (Ahmed, 2006). This also reaffirms the idea presented by Massey (1994) where the abstract notion of space is concrete as well as place. The imaginations of countries as behind, underdeveloped, sick, in transition, and so on. signal a way to imagine those spaces with specific characteristics. To make those characteristics "real" in place, subjects—such as those presented in this book—are incited to materialize abstract ideas of space into a body performing the imagination of that space. As Rajchman (1999) explains, the problem of minority is the problem of the concept of people outside the nation-state. He notes,

> . . . inventing a foreign or "minor" language within the languages supposed to secure the identities of national peoples; exposing other geographies not discernible within the borders, internal or external, of the "imagined communities" that nations were supposed to be—another time, another geography, another politics. (p. 50)

When asked about the reactions created out of these experiences of discrimination, the participant from Kenya declared:

> You know, these are identities, which have never been attached to me while I was in my country. Like, it would be out of proportion for anyone to even think of me stealing because of the class I belong to in my country, and at the same time, my moral standards and my way of life.

In another interview we continued discussing this idea of how international students are perceived by others at the University.

> To me the fact that I come from Africa makes it impossible for anybody to accept my true identity. So I feel bad, of course, since I know that I wouldn't convince anyone to see things through my lens. I see no point in doing so. But sometimes, I say, since I am here for only a short while, I don't care what anybody thinks or says about me while I am doing my business or without interfering with my business here. At home I am seen differently. The kinds of identities they put on me here would be unheard of in my country because of my status there, and my status is a university lecturer. So, people don't expect a university lecturer to be a thief, for instance, or to be a drug peddler, or to be a hungry person, lacking thought.

When talking about the possibility of being named in a different way and whether it would affect the way people talk about international students, this participant recalled a professor introducing him in a class:

> She [the professor] went on to say "he's a Fulbright student from Africa. He's doing these things, he's a professor there in Kenya in a university there." Things I didn't intend to say. I just said my name, my subject area, and the country where I come from. But she saw the need to introduce other forms of identity, like what type of student I am here...and what job I do in my country. And it influenced people's perceptions about me. So it is true the amount of description we give about our identity changes people's ideas about me, for instance, to include our social status at home, and our level of employment. Yes, but it does not change the wider picture. For instance, it won't stop them from referring to you as an international student. In my case, it won't stop the lady at University Clinic from thinking I'm sick.

From these excerpts it is clear to me that the discrete relations between places and subjectivities inhabiting those places are problematic. Places are made up through power relations, which construct the rules defining boundaries. These boundaries have the power to define the ways people belong to a place and at the same time the exclusions people may face (McDowell, 1999). These excerpts show how places are imagined as containers filled by subjects upon their arrival. Once you get to a place you wear the signs, symbols, and meanings constructed around people in relation to that place.

In contrast, following the idea that places are made up from the intersections of social relations of the subject inhabiting these places, needs to be understood in the same fluid and provisional dynamic. It is hard to think that subjects enter places as fixed and stable entities if indeed they and their interactions are producing the places themselves from the start (Massey, 2005).

Therefore, it is relevant in this discussion to ask questions about the predominant approach to understand international students' experiences. Location and positionality, as the figures of the static representations of place and space, have dominated discourses of international students both in policy and research studies. One should consider the ways international students are subjects conceptualizing and acting on different spatialities and are shifting critically within the places they inhabit. In such a fragile world of movement, space and place should be articulated in temporary moments of imagination.

One of the interesting points I want to highlight is the ways they talk about geography and home as scenes that anyone of us can find ourselves caught in. The stories told by this participant "...are opening stories that place the speaker in relation to others and the world and demonstrate an authority to speak as one who has 'been there' and been impacted or changed" (Stewart, 1996, p. 37).

SPACES HAPPEN

In this section, I intend to make the case of why notions of mobility and fluidity are preferable to alternative notions of stasis and fixity when talking about international students today. I want to argue that international students are *bodies in motion*, meaning that their experiences of movement are narratives of orientation and disorientation. Revisiting their narratives is required to better represent the challenges and experiences they live in the contemporary context of higher education. It is here, in the analysis of flux and fluidity, in ways of becoming rather than being, in the making and remaking of places, that movement between places can be seen as a force. I believe there is potential in exploring movement as a possibility to configure the self out of the imaginary of what we already know about subjectivities in relation to places. When one abandons traditional ways to interpret the self in relation to places, static cultural imaginaries are in question.

If the metaphor of movement serves to trouble taken-for-granted orientations toward spatial imaginaries, such as home, then understanding people's movements can say something about the problems of "following paths" when theorizing about their experiences. What path are we following when insisting on representing international students from Africa as sick people? And, to turn movement into a political feature we should pay attention to what Massumi reminds us: "All you need to do to avoid the path is, quoting Deleuze and Guattari: *look only at the movements*" (2002, p. 206).

Instead of viewing international students' subjectivities as attached to specific places I argue that they are a fluid combination of memories of places, constructed by and through episodes, several journeys, and the recreation of movements between and within places.

"Home," the imaginary idea of home provides a secure sense of telling yourself in a strange territory. Home is a temporal way to relate to the territory, to relate to what gives the sense of not only a stand-in for the nation, but a force that prevents from the feeling of lacking. Is there a differentiation possible between time and narrative? Is there a difference between the male body and the narration? Is there a difference between the African body and the narration? To envision a different way to tell time and space for international students I should suspend the African body. This means that I should not look at the African body as the extension of a territory, as the extension of a way to tell the correspondence between space and identity. Instead I should look for the voice of the African body, the ways times and spaces are expressed and the uses of them. As international students' experiences of times and spaces are fully contained within a language of the nation we need to find ways to suppress and complicate stories of supremacy in contexts of internationalization of higher education.

Thus, if places are made up from the intersections of social relations, then the subject inhabiting these places need to be understood in the same fluid and provisional dynamic. It is hard to think that subjects enter places with fixed and stable entities, if indeed they and their interactions are producing the places themselves in the first instance. The experiences lived by international students are relational and discourses-dependent; their lives are constrained by the rules and regulations of specific sites, which define their options and opportunities of being, and the ways they question the world. Being an international student is intrinsically related to places in a momentary and contradictory way. It is relevant in this discussion, therefore, to ask questions about the location and positionality of these communities in motion and to question why their stories have been ignored or not addressed properly in neither policies nor research studies. One should consider the way international students are subjects conceptualizing and acting on different places/spatialities and shifting silently within the places they inhabit. In such a fragile world of identity constitution, academics in transit are articulated in temporary moments of imagination.

Following this argument, I want to emphasize that universities have become a site that needs to be rethought and reassessed in the light of these new academic subjectivities. If social relations are the main constituents of a place, then it is relevant to ask what is it about universities that promote certain types of academic subjects to be talked about and to be educated? In what ways are universities sites of imagination and dreams for new academics? In what ways might these new narratives create new discourses or reinvent politics and practices within academia? Universities need to be rethought by the spread and re-creation of their relations.

In the rethinking of universities, perhaps it makes more sense to think about universities as a "meeting place." Massey (1994) argues that

> Most places have been these "meeting places"; even their "original inhabitants" usually came from somewhere else. This does not mean that the past is irrelevant to the identity of place. It simply means

that there is no internally produced, essential past. The identity of place, just as Hall argues in relation to cultural identity, is always and continuously being produced. Instead of looking back in nostalgia to some identity of place which it is assumed already exists, the past to be constructed. (p. 171)

Discourses of academics have frequently spoken to a naturalization of particular experiences within an implicit spatial frame of reference. Academics' attachments to places demand constant construction and reproduction of the meanings of place itself as well as their relation to it. A static conceptualization of place is therefore no longer a useful theoretical tool for *bodies in motion*.

By traveling, international students challenge and question the "notions of place as a source of belonging, identity, and security" (Massey, 1994, p. 170). This, when problematized, has an important impact on the relation of academics to disciplines and the epistemologies associated with specific knowledge terrains. Because of the increasing mobile composition of faculty within universities, I believe there has not been enough attention paid to the new possible discursive configurations of academia. Mobile subjectivities create new mappings for the configuration of universities. New practices created out of travel, mobility, and the recreation of places is forcing us to rethink new foundations from where to produce and recreate knowledge within the academic landscape.

Throughout these pages, I have presented some of the complexities of people moving through the interpretative frameworks of space/place, movement, and orientation, and exploring the possibilities for reimagining subjectivities in relation to places.

Drawing on the metaphors of space/place, movement, and orientation I have troubled the reproductive and performative dimension of places. From here I pose some questions: What is obscured by the traditional imagination of space and place? What is it that is reproduced when we rely on predetermined orientations to be followed?

Imagining Time and Space in Universities: Bodies in Motion creates new mappings for the configuration of universities. New practices created out of travel, mobility, and the recreation of places is forcing us to rethink "paths" followed by institutions.

...As to the questions of displacement and dislocation, loneliness and dissonance, the loss of balance and place...Many of us are vagabonds lost on a sea of dislocation. We look for safe harbours and places to go to a shore and explore...places and people where and with whom we can be ourselves. We wish to be in time, in rhythm with our thoughts and feelings...rather than on time.

CHAPTER 6

WOMEN AND TRAVEL: TEMPORAL IMAGINARIES OF BECOMING

The representation and uses of time have critical implications for the ways in which we orient discourses, practices, and bodies in institutions of higher education. Performing time in a taken-for-granted fashion incites practices of regulation, prescription, and limitation, which deserve to be talked about. In this chapter, I discuss the naturalization of time using the experiences of women who travel 'abroad' to obtain their graduate degrees and their subsequent narratives of "going back to their home countries." I seek to bring the discussion of time[1] to the forefront to explore the potential of ideas of becoming and of the new, particularly in times where the notions of fluidity, movement, and openness have been described as constituent elements of contemporary cultural and social life. The experiences of movement, dislocation, displacement, and reorientation lived by these women serve to explore the ways in which imagined notions of time support normalizing discourses and practices in academia.

In this chapter, I complicate the traditional understandings of movement as it has been characterized with metaphors of paths, and other signs of linearity and continuity, to analyze the experiences of women. I pursue the question whether it is possible to abandon the path, and if so, where we should be looking in order to recognize the dissonances and slippages.

Universities today, as active "players" within the global economy,[2] have pushed internationalization policies as a desirable standard to meet. In this environment, higher education institutions privilege the movement of students and academics. Academics' mobility and flexibility appear as directed toward convenient institutional ends, but with scarce problematization of the configuration of institutional practices of the experiences of "going abroad." Institutional discourses and policies ignore the "geopolitics of intellectual practices and their effect on other geographies, other people, and other cultures" (Sidhu, 2006, p. 61).

These academics' experiences of movement have been subjected to a number of concrete regulations such as visa restrictions, institutional commitments in their "home countries," among others. This means that the usual ways of claiming knowledge about their experiences are through already configured ideas of the immigrant, the foreigner, the journey, and the home, which are imagined as isolated and uncritical segments of the narration of "going abroad." However, such ideas might be seen instead as constitutive and reproductive dimensions of the meanings of these experiences.

The taken-for-granted institutional temporal imagination perceives these academics' experiences in a linear, predictable, and unproblematized manner: they go abroad, complete their degrees, and come back. This sounds as if it were possible "to claim a single universal duration" (Casey, 1999, p. 94) of the experiences of these people. In this linear and traditional way to give meaning to these experiences, time is understood as "divisible into a static past, a given present, and a predictable future" (Grosz, 1999, p. 9). In simple terms, this way of using time perpetuates static meanings of what it is to bring knowledge "back to the nation," and be an outsider. As a consequence it impedes, more productive imaginaries of becoming. These uses and representations of time not only perpetuate repetition and circularity of discourses of spatial orientations, nation, and instrumental knowledge in academia, but also deprive us of "becoming something other, we know not yet what" (Rajchman, 1999, p. 48). To think and perform time as a succession requires imagining and confining the self as *being someone we already know*, which is in need of questioning.

As a way to understand how traditional representations and uses of time operate in universities as we know them, concepts such as competitiveness in the market, self-regulatory/monitoring systems, efficiency, customer service, and the idea of internationalization need to be considered as part of the major discourses producing specific temporalities. Under the meta-discourse of market competitiveness, time is represented as a straight line that moves between two points. Direction and anticipation are possible only if I know what is coming next. Using Deleuze and Guattari's (1987) metaphor of space that comprises the idea of time, "the smooth and the striated [spaces] are distinguished first of all by an inverse relation between the point and the line (in the case of the striated, the line is between two points, while in the smooth, the point is between two lines)" (p. 480). In other words, the striated space represents the logical arrangement of trajectories where positions and locations are easily determined by a defined beginning and an end. Here time is understood as "divided into standard and standardizing units that are like snapshots of transition" (Massumi, 2002, p. 167). In the case of the smooth space, orientations are more fluid and not predefined by an already designed route or path. In this representation of space, time requires theorizing as an open-ended dimension.

In the case of striated space, time is a predictable pattern that provides an image of the world that can be presented, monitored, evaluated, and reproduced. In the case of the academic world, it represents a trace where straight lines are ready to be followed. As Deleuze and Guattari (1987) clarify when commenting on the difference between the figure of a map and a tracing: "What distinguishes the map from the tracing is that it [the map] is entirely oriented toward an experimentation in contact with the real. The map does not reproduce an unconscious closed in upon itself; it constructs the unconscious" (p. 12). They go further: "A map has multiple entryways, as opposed to the tracing, which always comes back 'to the same'. The map has to do with performance, whereas the tracing always involves an alleged 'competence'" (p. 13). These ways of imagining experiences using a linear representation of time link meanings, subjectivities and practices to previous and already established ways of being, knowing, and behaving. As Derrida (cited in Lather, 2007, p. 15) expresses, "...when the path is given…the decision is already made" (p. 15). As I mentioned before, such normative narratives of time are at the center of nearly every definition and practice in higher education. For instance, the use of the discourse of quality assurance to govern higher education is based on the logic of standards, which set a specific point of departure and arrival for processes and practices in higher education. Once these departure and arrival points have been set up, institutional efforts are directed toward meeting those ends. This implies a singular and specific way to imagine, inhabit, and perform institutional time. Moreover, market-based orientations and managerial accountability systems also shape subject's sense and experience of time. The discourse of the expert, as an external entity that monitors and surveils the functioning of others in higher education, prevents spontaneity, nonlinear behaviors, and favors the circularity of homogeneity, repetition, and regularity. As Lyotard (1979) reminds us, "The decision makers…attempt to manage these clouds of sociality according to input/output matrices, following a logic which implies that their elements are commensurable and that the whole is determinable. They allocate our lives for the growth of power…[and] the legitimation of that power is based on its optimizing the system's performance-efficiency" (p. xxiv).

These temporal patterns described above incite specific ways to read women academics' experiences of going abroad to earn their graduate degrees, which are confined to already-made imaginations of ways of doing, behaving, and inhabiting institutional spaces. Interesting enough is how universities address the return of these academics under the discourse of "academic reinsertion." Under practices of institutional reinsertion that indicate from where to start, where to go, and how to behave, it is interesting to ask how academic subjectivities exercise and practice this conditioned autonomy and authenticity. The ways these women talk about their experiences are crucial to permit the questioning of the perseverance of certain temporal imaginaries (such as the *returning professor*) that reassert specific academic identities premised on essentialized notions of time. To imagine the knower and what she/he does under this a-political notion of time sustains an unquestionable set of practices and meanings in higher education institutions.

It is in this context that this chapter problematizes how intellectual practices of travel have been normalized by traditional understandings of time having critical implications such as the repetition and circulation of normative ideas and practices in academia. To trouble normative ways of using time in universities requires the uses of time as a force, which means that time can be thought as something else (Grosz, 1999; Deleuze and Guattari, 1987) other than the locked-in idea of the succession of specific units. Therefore, one of the goals of this chapter is to use these narratives of academics who travel "abroad" to question the "promise of the new" (Grosz, 1999). As Elizabeth Grosz (1999) proposes, to rethink "temporality in terms of the surprise of the new, the inherent capacity for time to link in extraordinarily complex ways the past and present to a future that is uncontained by them and has the capacity to rewrite and transform them" (p. 7).

I use excerpts from interviews with women academics in Chile from two different universities to show how the uses of time sustain, and probably revitalize, neutral and universal discourses of spatial orientations, the nation, and instrumental knowledge. The chosen interviews are part of a larger project whose purpose was to understand uses of policies and practices of internationalization of higher education in Chile. As discussed earlier, internationalization discourses in universities have become a major producer of specific ways to imagine not only global and local space, but also time and movement. I interviewed 30 women in multiple disciplines, including natural sciences, social sciences, humanities, and arts, who obtained their graduate degrees in Australia, the United States, England, and Spain. A substantial dimension of the internationalization initiatives in higher education institutions are oriented to "sending" and "receiving" students and academics to and from different parts of the world. As expected, Chilean universities are mimicking the global tendency to foster movement of academics as highly desirable to respond to "global standards" that construct mobility as a characteristic of "global times," and as a source of privilege and important means to increase economic resources for the institution.

When reading the interviews I was interested in what may seem repetitive and taken-for-granted as these women narrate their experiences of going back to their institutions. In reading the interviews some of the questions that came to my mind were:

How do these women use ideas of time and what do these ideas reiterate? How do the uses of time serve the stabilization of neutral discourses in academia?. And finally, how does time, as a force, offer a way to think about the *becoming* and *the new*?

In the following pages, I discuss the uses of time and its functioning as a frame to reproduce discourses of nation, progress, and instrumental knowledge. I focus on the ways in which women narrate their experiences of *going abroad* and *coming back* in relation to the production of narratives of spatial orientations, the perseverance of the idea of the nation, and the reproduction of the notion of neutral knowledge. The reiteration of these ideas demands a constant affirmation of time as a way of passing, and the knower as someone we already know. I intend to show that these people's narratives offer a critical scenario to talk about how the tenacious hold of the language of traditional time revitalizes the neutral and universalized understanding of how we inhabit places, reproduces practices of a contained self, and repeats unquestionable essentialisms.

SPATIAL ORIENTATIONS-MAPPING TIMES

How narratives of linear time relate to specific orientations toward geographical and institutional spaces represented by the interviewees' experiences are explored. There is a distinct boundary made by these academics between the self and the world, that in many ways are products of normative ideas of time. These ways of confining experiences to a certain logic of time creates ideas of space as containers of happenings, and by doing this, reaffirms specific orientations toward objects and practices. This establishes and formalizes a way to behave in institutions, allowing specific understandings of what "counts" as experiences of "going abroad" and "coming back." The idea of space presented by the participants through their narratives suggests that space is inhabited by "things"; therefore, the possibility of change and movement is only an attribute of time. For instance, one of the participants mentions that "[...] the process of coming back does not happen, and if it happens, you are all the time tumbling, the only

thing that you want is to come back to where you come from [...]
I came back [to Chile] three years ago, but the truth is that I came
back only a couple of months ago." The idealized process of "coming
back" expressed by this participant seems problematic. Expectations
about the institutional meanings of their *returning* processes show the
dissonances between what has happened to them in time and what is
not absorbed by the place they inhabit. What I think it is interesting
is how the construction of a static, contained past offers a specific way
to imagine the relation between the academic and the institutional
space. To imagine spaces as absolute containers of experiences suggests that time reflects a *past* only possible to be accounted for. This
kind of subjection to places, depending on specific ways to imagine
time, requires a specific subject, a subject who is determined to *be* the
teller of that past and the promoter of the predictable future based on
that history.

The ways these women construct ideas of time as a way to re-orient
themselves to geographic experiences have something to say about
the possibilities of imagining themselves as something else, not yet
to be known. To "come back," as expressed by these women, involves
a nostalgic account of the past. As this woman orients herself toward
time as central to her experiences, space becomes a passive construction to be inhabited. What matters here is what it does to imagine
space as subjected to time. As Sarah Ahmed (2006) points out, "To
be oriented around something means to make that thing central, or as
being as the center of one's being or action" (p. 116).

Another participant shows how the representation of space is subjected to imaginations of time, "...what happens is that the institution remains immune to the changes experienced by the academic
after four or five years being abroad. So a struggle starts between
what I hope is going to happen after coming back and what really
happens, and that is hard to bear." The passivity of space against the
idea of an active time, as where experiences actually happen, is a problematic construction mainly because it dissociates and depolitizes the
past in relation to the present. To grant the past the possibility to
disappear, to no longer act, is a way to maintain the neutrality of institutional spaces. Institutions remain untouched by the complex experiences of travel. Taken-for-granted ideas of time and space allow the

reproduction and repetition of subjectivities, meanings, symbols, and practices. As Elizabeth Grosz (1995) reminds us, "The kinds of world we inhabit, and our understandings of our places in these worlds are to some extent an effect of the ways in which we understand space and time" (p. 97).

What most of these narratives do is to reaffirm representations of a past, present, and future as divisible and self-contained. This notion of time creates an absolute space, a "spatialization of time" (Grosz, 1999, p. 6), which incites the proliferation of other discourses, such as nation and instrumental knowledge, and revitalizes an unquestionable separation between geographies, which reproduces essentialisms and hierarchies of power. Neil Smith and Cindi Katz (1993) explain that "it is not space per se that expresses power, but the thoroughly naturalized absolute conception of space that grew up with capitalism" (p. 76), which indicates that money (along with race, gender, sexuality, etc.) dictates access and therefore determines the experience of space. The "absoluteness of space" (Smith and Katz, 1993) expressed by the participants of this study appears equally impossible to question. For instance, one of the participants comments when describing her experience being abroad:

> I think it is very important that we can look at our country with a more international perspective. To do what you have to do in order to earn certain standards, if not, we [meaning Chile] stay too isolated, and we will be perceived as a small little town. It is important to observe situations from the outside. From the outside you can observe the good and the bad of your country. I think the world is not in a moment where we can choose to live in isolation.

The repetition of geographic representations such as "outside" and "inside," "abroad" and "home country," shows the persistence of essentialist ideas involved in the construction of spaces. These oppositional ways of perceiving and representing spaces have succeeded through a specific understanding of time. To imagine time as a sequence of pieces and experiences reinforces the imagination of space as the container of those pieces. Doreen Massey (1993) reminds us, "Over and over again, time is defined by such things as change, movement, history, dynamism; while space, rather lamely by comparison, is simply the absence of those things" (p. 148). To experience space as a reservoir of contacts, symbols, and meanings suggests that people "arrive" to a predefined set of practices that require accommodation to be lived. In this notion of time dislocated from space, time becomes a way of passing, producing depoliticized spaces. Women academics' going back experiences are fabricated around these atemporal ideas of space.

As an example of the spatialized construction of these experiences (Laclau, cited in Massey, 1993) another participant eloquently expresses: "Chile is perceived as a place away from the world, away from the places where things really happen, away from the First World." What these ideas do is to naturalize the relationship between space and time reinforcing a "position-gridded space" (Massumi, 2002, p. 15). As a consequence of this spatial and temporal orientation, other constructs, such as nation, become revitalized.

THE NATION-REVITALIZED

My argument in this section is that the essentialized ideas of the nation sustained by these participants have, as antecedents, the separation of time and space, where time is claimed to be a dimension governing the construction of essential spaces. Time, as a divisible past, present, and future, creates specific ways to imagine the nation, which in turn produces specific practices and languages for women in academia, such as nationalisms and patriotic impulses. For instance, Alarcon et al. (1999), when discussing the transnational subjects of feminist movements, note that international movement "[...] relies on and reinforces the discrete nature of the nation, reifying and mystifying the historical phenomenon of the modern state" (p. 13).

In the case of the interviewees' narratives, there is a repetitive disposition to talk about the nation as an entity in need of constant reconstruction. One participant notes:

[...] it is not only to bring knowledge from the outside. It also has to do with the fact that we go outside and show what we are doing. We need to be that bridge within Latin America, in other words, I want to believe that the processes of internationalization contribute to the fostering of our identity.

Following the same nationalistic tone, another interviewee suggests, "...at the end you are representing a country. You arrive to this other country and nobody knows a thing about Chile. At least, this is what happens to Chile because it is a far away country, you are not representing [just] yourself, you represent a community." The self-identity of the nation requires duties and responsibilities to be performed. The sense of belonging and the desire to bind oneself to territories are produced and reproduced through the insistence of the notion of a community and the unified identity of a group. The discourse of ambassadors, used in the rhetorics on internationalization of higher education, sustains the notion that the subject is a container of a representation of the place she/he inhabits.

As academics moving to complete their degrees there is a wide range of discourses associated. The idea of the ambassador is contrasted by the brain drain. For instance, one of the participants state that when thinking of going abroad for graduate studies, sponsored by countries different than the home country, there is a fear that these academics will become "experts" in issues pertaining to the interests of the other nations, which leads her to then say, "every time you are making decisions that distance you from Chile, and you get integrated to another country's interests, it is one lost brain for Chile."

As these women start experiencing gendered, disciplinary, and institutional constraints once they are "back," the normalized construction of a nation becomes a way to sustain a certain stability in order to represent their experiences of being "abroad." This produces problematic imaginations of the relations between the knower and the purposes of knowing. Knowledge serves to sustain and bind the imagination of a nation and a unitary identity. In so many ways, as territory is related to the idea of belonging, knowledge is also experienced as belonging to specific territories.

In a different reading of these experiences, one could argue that they produce a deterritorialization of the knower, but this occurs at the same time the experiences of being outside reterritorialize the knower (Deleuze and Guattari, 1987). As Deleuze and Guattari (1987) explain, "reterritorialization must not be confused with a return to a primitive or older territoriality: it necessarily implies a set of artifices by which one element, itself deterritorialized, serves as a new territoriality for another, which has also lost its territoriality as well" (p. 174). For example, in the case of these women's experiences, the idea of nation (always slippery) acts as the meaningful signifier from where to reterritorialize the knower, but at the same time, it creates a strong revitalization of the meaning of the nation itself. What is reproduced is the fiction of a nation as an entity that demands particular identities and communities in order to survive and compete with other nations within the world economy. The idea of the nation revitalizes itself with renewed meanings. For instance, one of the participants notes that

> ...to go abroad does not guarantee that you are going to be better [...]. What I think is good is to have the capacity to experience going abroad but to focus your research interests in Chile, do you understand what I am saying? In other words, to take the US or European experiences to improve your research methods and procedures, theoretical frameworks, etc., but I think that your research interests must be located in Chile.

In a different interview, a participant recalls, "I had the chance to go back to Australia, but I did not feel motivated, because I always thought that the knowledge you get, being a little bit patriotic, you have to use it to improve something in Chile." As I mentioned before, these academic's specific ways to orient themselves to geographical spaces in relation to knowledge reproduces and circulates essentialized constructions of identities and national territories. Knowledge is used to reproduce the fiction of the nation. These women's narratives indicate their desire to retain a national identity; at the same time, they invoke boundaries and express good intentions directed at the well-being of the nation. All these facilitate new expressions of nationalist sentiments generated by the logics of academic travel. As Benedict Anderson (cited in Weinbaum, 2007) argues, "nations are brought into being by peoples whose access to print culture enables collective imagination of involvement in political and cultural projects that extends back into a 'immemorial past' and 'glides into a timeless future'" (p. 167). Women's narratives embody the future of the nation.

As Pheng Cheah (1999) contends, "the nation, in other words, guarantees an eternal future" (p. 177). To desire and imagine the permanency of a nation suggests that the past precedes the present. In these women's narratives, the future of the nation is constructed through the image of a specific kind of knowledge, a kind of knowledge that does not dialogue with the world around it, a knowledge that follows the game of a dual temporality, that is past and future. To rely on practices of guarding the future of the nation and the stability of the institution is a way for these women to be academically intelligible. This, of course, resonates with traditional stories of subordination of women, which can be understood as a reinscription of masculine practices.

When analyzing academics' narratives, ideas of the nation, space, geography, and/or territory are treated as a structure to sustain. And, as many scholars have noted, women's commitment to the building of the nation has different venues to be expressed. For example, Alys Eve Weinbaum (2007) suggests that "…men and women participate differently in nation-building and that reproductive heterosexuality plays a decisive role in the creation of nationalist ideologies, which are, in turn deeply gendered and heteronormative" (p. 169). Women contribute actively

> in nationalist struggles for liberation; as mothers, the biological reproducers of subjects and national populations; as upholders of the boundaries of nations through restrictions on reproductive sexuality and the circumscription of marriage within ethnic and racial groups; as teachers and transmitters of national culture; and as symbolic signifiers of nations. (Yuval-Davis and Anthias, cited in Weinbaum, 2007, p.167)

Normative time uses and reuses existing gender hierarchies to reproduce ideas of the nation, notions of attachment, and the need to protect an imagined community. At the same time, the idea of the nation normalizes time, which consequently reiterates practices of submission to the already-given. These nationalist constructions unfold other connected discourses such as the proliferation of instrumental knowledge, as the thing that can move across geographies.

KNOWLEDGE TRAVELS

My interest here is to discuss how academic women situate themselves in institutional practices and how knowledge can be talked about in a way that reflects and includes the breakdowns in representing the experiences of going abroad. What do the uses of time (as we know it) do to the practices and meanings of *doing* knowledge?

The ways these women talk about politics and representations of knowledge when returning offers a possibility to trouble what it is repeated and revitalized by discourses of globalization and objectified knowledge. Knowledge takes the figure of a product mobilized between spaces. When knowledge comes to be a part of the equation, academics do not *do knowledge*, they acquire it, and make it travel, and be spread. The academics' narratives show the repetition of neutral ideas of knowledge and how they help preserve authoritarian practices in higher education. For these people, who have gone through processes of deterritorialization and reterritorialization (Deleuze and Guattari, 1987), the past, as part of the becoming of the knower, is bracketed or set aside. The past can be told as an experience to be recounted but it is not told as an interruption to how they know. What interests me is that most of their narratives express a desire to be intelligible, institutionally speaking. And apparently to achieve this, they "...need to repeat the familiar and normalized" (Lather, 2007, p.39). The contradictions lived by these women are diverse; for instance, one of the participants eloquently expresses, "you come back with the feeling that you want to share all you've learned, but when you get back it does not work like this and this is the moment in time when you start feeling contradicted and scared." These expressions of anxiety around their institutional experiences show some of the reactions to the dissonances they go through. Most of the images associated with international movement in academia relate to an elite travel. Those who are entitled to move across geographies because of their research are positioned in particular social and cultural places. This becomes confusing.

Another way to understand the ways these women proliferate ideas of knowledge as something people mobilize between places is related to discourses that insist on academic performance, auditing, and accountability. Under these discourses knowledge needs to be represented as *something* in order to be accounted for. As a consequence, this representation of knowledge neutralizes the complexities of what it means to be an academic constructing knowledge in a context of global movement. In this way of understanding knowledge, "...a person does not have to know how to be what knowledge says [s]he is" (Lyotard, 1979, p. 26).

Another interesting point one of the participants makes is how creating knowledge while abroad is perceived as an open, creative, and transformative experience. She states: "...to go abroad helps you abandon a more traditional way of thinking." My question here is what kind of knowledge or way of knowing is abandoned, to what extent, and until when? If *going abroad* invokes a past, a different way of doing, then, when they return, they become encapsulated in tradition, whatever that means. They come back to the limits imposed by disciplines and institutions. If I follow what Grosz (2005) explains, "... [past and present] exist, they 'occur' at the same time. The past and present are created simultaneously" (p. 103), then what are those forces that incite these women to conform to and repeat frames of references, spatial divisions of experiences, and to confine themselves to imaginations of time? If time were conceptualized and imagined in a different way, as "not simply mechanical repetition, the causal effects of objects on objects, but the indeterminate, the unfolding and the emergence of the new" (Grosz, 2005, p. 110), the dialogue between those experiences that reconstruct a past as static with the refiguration of the new, of the not-yet-to become, would require different discourses about what is to be known and the knower.

The ways they construct their experiences of *return* reflect not only a return to a specific place left behind, but also a return to foundations, to referents, to the ways they used to *do knowledge*. Another participant expresses her frustration when talking about the sacralization of disciplines and what it does to her present work. She states:

> In Social Sciences there is an academic dialogue but it is restricted because of the disciplinary limits. Somehow the college urges, implicitly, to use the theoretical assumptions pertaining to the disciplines

you are in (psychology, sociology, or social work) and, when the disciplinary fields get integrated, a delegitimation is produced. For instance, I have been presenting my research advances to some of my colleagues using concepts that do not belong to psychology and they do not understand me, or they resist understanding. That is very serious to me.

This rigidity raises critical questions about how the experiences of going abroad in relation to knowledge complicate the politics of knowledge in universities. It is like knowledge is already set as a path to follow, as a strict line that guides and orients bodies, practices, and imaginaries. If it is so, experiences of going abroad and coming back for these women academics are decisions already made. It is, as Brian Massumi (2002) expresses, "if you know where you will end up when you begin, nothing has happened in the meantime" (p. 18).

These passages show the dependence created around traditional conceptual systems that dictate a way to behave and follow already authorized paths. The repetition of institutional and disciplinary constructions assures and protects the continuum, the stability of knowledges, the definition of the objects to know, and certainly, the identity of the knower. Sidhu (2006) explains,

> Only certain objects are talked about and then only certain ways within disciplinary paradigms. Historically, the discourses of women, indigenous people, and many non-Western people, along with other minorities, have been constructed as irrational, and their knowledges subsequently subordinated. Overall, the rules of discourse contribute toward a tendency by disciplines to remain fixed in time and space. (p. 33)

In this case, women's aspirations take shape as the result of limits. The way they understand and interpret knowledge normalizes their subjectivities. They subject themselves to what is already given. Also, as Lyotard (1979) reminds us,

> we know today that the limits the institution imposes on potential language 'moves' are never established once and for all (even if they have been formally defined). Rather, the limits are themselves the stakes and

provisional results of language, strategies, within the institutions and without. (p. 17)

Women's representations of knowledge tell me that there are at least two ways in which they imagine what they do. One is unquestioned, imposed, technocratized, unscrutinized, institutionalized. The other is something they have to struggle for, not recognized, invalidated, and more creative. This may be connected to what Lyotard (1979) describes as scientific knowledge and narrative knowledge. He explains, "In the first place, scientific knowledge does not represent the totality of knowledge; it has always existed in addition to, and in competition and conflict with another kind of knowledge, which I will call narrative in the interest of simplicity" (p. 7). What these women describe as a complex practice of creating knowledge when they are back tells about their involvement in both the normalization and revitalization of practices of power.

As an example of the critical meanings of knowledge one interviewee explains:

> If you work around problematic issues such as the HIV you have to name them in a different way. I have modified my research a little bit because I am part of this institution (religious institution) and, the truth is that it hasn't been an obstacle to do my work. In fact, my work is very complicated from a religious perspective and I have never seen a closed door.

The same participant in a different line notes,

> At one point we had to talk to one religious authority, because of our research study on issues of sexuality. We had to explain that we were aware that the topic was a sensitive one and this person gave us his support. The only thing he requested was discretion, in the sense that not to be public and appear in newspapers as faculty members of the X University.

The ways these women revitalize normative practices of knowledge creation guarantee the identity of the knower as apolitical. Institutions dictate the kind of research to be done and the ways it should be communicated.

In another example, a participant who speaks as a member of a religious institution expresses:

> well, for instance, there is a very interesting discussion about the uses of the morning-after pill. As you may imagine, there are institutional effects because of the topic. I talk as a religious person and I value my position. But in this case, it is the same when we talk about abortion or the divorce law, by teaching the students about divorce, it does not mean that we favor divorce.

The lack of politics of knowledge produced by the idea that knowledge is something people move around, not something that people *do,* resonates with the detachment produced by the uses of time understood as discrete units of succession (past, present, and future). This way to understand and give meaning to knowledge confines the self as a predictable subjectivity who *reinserts* her/himself into already existing institutions and disciplines.

In a different but related dimension, these women talk about their experiences of institutional exclusion. One of them states:

> Sometimes I have the impression that these dynamics of discrimination are produced because I am perceived as a menace because of the new knowledge I bring, and the new ways I have to work. This is one of the reasons why it is so hard to find an academic space when you are back.

Again, knowledge as a practice constitutes a way to differentiate what these women do from institutional practices. The experiences of constructing knowledge in a more open, creative, and political manner make these people question the institutional present and the precautions they have to face. For instance, another participant expresses some kind of confusion when trying to explain why her academic activities have not been as successful as she expected: "I have like six papers in process, I even have the tables with results, but I still cannot sit down and write. Now, as I told you, it may be something related to my personality, I am not sure, but there are some people who do it anyway, so I think that it is because I tried to do only the hours I am paid for."[3] As might be predictable, one of the participants questions the fact of being a woman and she states: "[the fact of being a woman]...does not assure that whatever you say is going to be accepted, but I do believe that going abroad helps you having a healthy self-steem, right?" In these two comments, the lack of politics to interpret the institutional experiences they go through speaks about the representations of institutional spaces as a container of meanings and symbols to where they "arrive." This depolitization of institutional knowledge incites them to repeat traditional uses of power (e.g. gender, sexuality, race, etc.) in a noncritical manner. As international movement is interpreted as a way to gain academic and professional status, for women to work on self-esteem issues tells about gender and the differences to experience the purposes of movement. Gender hierarchies reproduce specific ways to narrate international movement with political consequences.

What is particularly interesting is the propensity of these women to conform and follow the comfortable (even gender is narrated as a comfortable position). It is as if they discipline themselves to forge the idea of stability and institutional obedience. As Grosz explains when describing Deleuze' worries about the production of the new (1995), "It is as if the forces of knowledge and power cannot tolerate difference, the new, the unthought, the outside, and do all that they can to suppress it, force it to conform to expectation, to fit into a structure, be absorbable, assimilable, and digestible without disturbance or perturbation" (p. 130). And these women act as if they believe the same.

TIME, WOMEN

The circulation and repetition of normalized discourses presented by these women's narratives illustrate the persuasive force of time—time as a way of passing that acts upon us and goes beyond our control. To think and perform time as a succession requires the confirmation of the self as someone we already know. Time works as a trace, as a line to follow, a pattern to revitalize. From this point of view, women academics will always come back to *the same*. If time is understood this way to explain what is happening to these women, then time becomes a performance that entails a *being* (different from becoming), a subjectivity we already know.

When Elizabeth Grosz (2005) discusses Deleuze and Bergson's ideas about life, duration, and history, she says that these ideas "... are never either a matter of unfolding and already work out blueprint or simply the gradual accretion of qualities which progress stage by stage of piecemeal over time" (p. 111). In this chapter, time has been posed as a question, and as a possibility to interrupt the preconceived notions of who we are and what we do.

Time, traditionally imagined as mechanical repetition, functions in implicit ways. As Grosz (1999) explains, "(time) tends to function as a silent accompaniment, a shadowy implication underlying, contextualizing, and eventually undoing all knowledges and practices without being their explicit object of analysis or speculation" (p. 1). The collective imagination of time as intangible neutralizes the notion of time as a force of becoming. If time works as the silent entity behind our representations, it must also work as a force. As Bergson explains (cited in Grosz, 2005), time also incites "the indeterminate, the unfolding and the emergence of the new: 'Time is something. Therefore it acts. Time is what hinders everything from being given at once. It retards, or rather it is retardation. It must therefore be elaboration'" (p. 110).

What I have done in this chapter is to trouble potential *becomings* through the experiences of travel of women academics. To conceptualize time as becoming means that we have to interrupt the reduction of time as the frame that dictates temporal orders (e.g. casuality). Time as becoming is "as an opening up which is at the same time a form of bifurcation or divergence" (Grosz, 1999, p. 4). In this sense, time is seen as the possibility of the new, of the unpredictable. Elizabeth Grosz (1999) when discussing the work of Nietzsche, Deleuze, and Bergson, states that "it is significant that this future-oriented temporality brings with it the centrality of the concept of chance, of what is in principle unpredictable, is of the essence of a time that is not regulated by causality and determination but unfolds with its own rhythms and logic, its own enigmas and impetus" (p. 4). To imagine and perform time this way implies that the knower is open to the unpredictability of the future, to experience becoming someone else, someone she/he does not know. This also brings the possibility of unfolding complex experiences of knowing. As Grosz (1999) argues, "We cannot know what the new will bring, what the promise of the future is for us: to know the future is deny it as future, to place it as a given, as past" (p. 6). By exploring the representations and uses of time of these women academics, it is clear to me that the power of traditional ideas of time prevent people from the new and the surprise of the unknown. Their narratives portray a highly stable definition of time as succession, which is based on the idea that past-present-future are separated and independent segments of a trace. In this imaginary, the self is restricted to perform and embody the characteristics of each portion of the trace: past as a given, present as the transition to what is next, and future as the consolidation of the anticipation grounded in the present. To naturalize these temporal dimensions implies erasing the knower from the known, and impeding anything that relates to the "yet-to-come." If time were seen as a force that incites an unknown future, a future with no linear precedents, how would these women's narratives look? What if we actualize the idea of time? How would new thinking of time transform the relations between travel, internationalization, and knowledge?

The imaginations of these women about who they are and what they do reflect habits of memory. The repetition of pasts in the presents signals the reproduction of the same, of what we already know. Therefore, concepts and meanings such as nation, will continue being stuck on time. The reinvention of time as an open-ended dimension transforms political and cultural imaginations of ideas of internationalization and travel in academia.

Time as becoming resonates with other concepts such as openness, randomness, the yet-to-come, the new. Elizabeth Grosz (1999) when discussing the approaches of *time as difference* explains, "...each in his way [referring to Deleuze, Bergson, and Nietzsche] affirms time as open-ended and fundamentally active force—a materializing if not material—force whose movements and operations have an inherent element of surprise, unpredictability, or newness" (p. 4). If uses of time resonate more with indeterminacy of the future, in what ways are the past and present in dialogue with the knower and what is to be known? Perhaps discourses of internationalization and movement of academics will not be oriented to only "secure *the* truth, but to explore the dimensions of the multiple forms of knowing and practices by which truths are ascertained" (Alcoff, 1999, p. 75).

Time, as a force, offers the possibility to think who we are and what we do otherwise: To think the new, to allow the unexpected to unfold, to provoke the unpredictable. These women academics' stories show how the unconscious uses of time reiterates essentialisms and ways of doing. The predictability, anticipated duration, and already-worked-out temporalities of these women's experiences show that time (as we know it) works as another strategic effect of self-regulation. To trouble the regularity of their temporal movement and meanings attached to their experiences seems important particularly if they are related to other constructions (space, nation, and knowledge) that are in need of reimagining.

My aim here has been to mobilize my own way to think time. These women experiences helped me to imagine the "knower to come," and to imagine the reinvention of the time of the travel. Time has served as a framework to question those impulses that go beyond our control that impede us to think otherwise.

CHAPTER 7

WOMEN AND THE POLITICS OF WRITING*

This chapter reveals much of the interests and motivations behind the writing of this book. It seeks to stimulate a discussion on the forces that come to play when talking about the production of knowledge in universities understood as international identities particularly through the act of writing. As I have laid out along the book, contemporary ways to reason universities as international institutions have important effects on the configuration of knowledge, academic subjectivities, and their relations. As expected, such new configurations or ways to frame international practices and discourses for universities require a close examination. Discourses of internationalization of higher education that use institutional arrangements to promote specific practices in order to name themselves as successfully international (such as international networks and circuits to publish academic work, designing and implementing international collaborative research, high level of indexed publications, and so on) produce the idea that all these are the "natural" institutional outcomes and aspirations for professors. New ways to push universities to be part of the "knowledge society" discourse are deployed in particular and invisible practices of regulation that assume and promote specific academic identities.

These institutional practices create the conditions for a new institutional developmentalism (Sidhu, 2007) where the reconfiguration of international practices has taken the role of managerial tools. Such is the case of institutional pressure for publications in those journals subscribed to the ISI and SCOPUS databases, which have critical impacts on the nature of writing in academia.* Besides, creating the collective idea that these writing and publishing practices represent the totality and desirable outcome, it produces an ethical gap where it is necessary for some research to be aligned with the market's requirements. These frames to produce knowledge have taken dangerous turns, as Minnich (2005) notes,

> Public universities are taking funds from corporations to support research, which those corporations then control lest potentially profitable findings leak to competitors. As a result, some scholarly gatherings and peer-reviewed journals are seen not as guardians of sound scholarship for the public good, but as threats to future corporate profits (in which universities increasingly yearn to share). (p. 9)

Beyond taking up the ethical problems about this way of framing the relation between universities and corporations, I want to focus my analysis on how this new framing of development in higher education institutions is shaping the identity of those who work there.

It is my contention that contemporary institutional cultures produced through these discourses privilege the constitution of a disembodied academic subjectivity that requires subjects to narrate themselves with no reference to gendered, racialized, nationalized, and sexualized categories. I agree with Sidhu and Dall'Alba (2012) who note that "disembodiment is a political technology to install the 'naturalness' and unproblematic nature of 'globalization' and global education market" (p. 414). What I want to explore in this chapter are the ways disembodiment is visible when women describe their practices of writing. I want to present how women's stories of writing practices are full of contradictions that make possible talking about the politics of producing knowledge (Haraway, 1988) in universities today. In many ways, to produce knowledge and accounts of life in writing "despite the constraints of the body is not possible" (Merleau Ponty,1962/1945, cited in Sidhu and Dall'Alba, 2012, p. 416).

It is exactly through the spatial and temporal understandings of our body that we come to know. Gender, sexuality, age, skin color are particular positions that allow us to tell specific stories of the world. To explore the ways professors are affected by their bodies and if they comply (or not) to institutional mandates of productivity and the production of the new arrangements in academia is a way to question the contemporary prescriptions for universities.

Exploring how disembodiment is narrated and lived by women through their acts of academic writing, particularly in disciplines related to Humanities and Social Sciences, is a way to locate "right here" what is prescribed "out there." Ignoring the stories women provide for understanding the political complexities of academic writing today is a way to disseminate the idea that one way of valuing and practicing writing fits all equally. The expectation that these institutional demands (publishing in specific journals, and as a consequence to write for a specific audience with a specific tone) fit all is contradictory to what the stories women tell. In the current international context, movement of bodies and knowledges affect the present demands for universities. I sustain that it is exactly in this context that "embodiment, [works as] a condition for knowing; it makes knowing possible" (Sidhu and Dall'Alba, 2012, pp. 416). Permanent movement and fluidity of questionings of who we are occupying different spaces and living different times, our bodies and how they are conditioned are key for the production and circulation of knowledge.

As institutionalized discourses of academic productivity have forged powerful ideas about what kind of academics' work and practices should be rewarded, academia has become a site of anxious production of those who act out the norm and those who are left behind. This normalizing power of discourses of academic productivity creates specific circuits of privilege in universities (Mills, 1997). Even though this is not a new distinction, I believe these normalizing discourses have come to operate in different registers. These discourses have entered into the ordinary world of academia and as such, those spaces of counterproduction of knowledge have come to have different tones. Under these conditions to produce the successful academic trajectory I believe we have to pay attention to the small-scale ways professors narrate what they do, how they talk about their teaching and their writing. What are the current ways professors use to talk about their teaching and writing?

Of course, this new way to frame and justify this updated distinction of "we/they" (meaning the successful and nonsuccesful academic) in universities refers to modernist ideals of rationality and order, which are successfully reinforced by contemporary market assumptions. These assumptions are oriented to uphold the idea that "the market" operates as a neutral entity and therefore its prescriptions are unquestionable. This is a productive way to differentiate academic identities, formalize different statuses for knowledges, and make recognizable the intimate practices that are discarded as nonproductive. What matters to me is how writing as an intimate practice is subjected to normalizing practices.

> The body of the academic, like that any other modern citizen, has been normalized—measured, cataloged, segmented, and examined—through disciplinary discourses. Such practices work to eliminate risk inasmuch as risk means the real possibility of mistake, error, and failure. This is not simply failure to complete a particular task to an acceptable standard, but, [...] failure to produce oneself as a reasoning, reasonable citizen: and it is this possibility that makes risk taking so serious. (McWilliam, 2000, p. 169)

In this scenario, some of the questions that orient my analysis are as follows: What kind of identities and notions of space and time are universities scripting for themselves in order to succeed in this highly competitive international education market? In what ways does embodiment allow questioning of dominant understandings of the space and time of academic writing? In other words, how are contemporary discourses of academic productivity embodied performances that orient academics to specific questionings about the intimate? How do these circumstances in which they are pushed to "produce" affect what they write? And most importantly, how does what we politically understand as writing affect who we become?

WAYS TO REASON UNIVERSITIES

As internationalization of higher education discourses promote, solidify, and reward university practices that focus on innovation, patenting, curriculum standardization, competencies, accreditation, and so on, all of them broadcasted as new, they become unquestionable desirable institutional goals. As an extension, institutional cultures have become strongly affected by discourses that privilege the proliferation of practices of instrumentalization of knowledge and the promotion of entrepreneurial academic subjectivities (Sidhu, 2006; Davidson-Harden, 2009; Peters, 1992, 2002, Lee Carlson, 2009). In many different ways, discourses of internationalization of higher education have come to serve neoliberal practices in universities, in turn affecting their social missions, academic priorities, and organizational structures.

Major discourses in the meanings of universities today are strongly connected to the reconceptualization of knowledge as a trade commodity and as a response to the market's needs. This has important effects on the ways identities are produced and on the purposes of fostering specific practices. Such logics are upheld by a blind trust in the capacity of markets to orient and organize social and cultural aspects of universities in such a way that it is hard to notice. For instance, the ways commodification of knowledge is strongly connected to the competitiveness of nation-states because of their capacities in knowledge production, is part of the popular discourse today. As Bill Readings notes (1996),

> ...the University is becoming a different kind of institution, one that is no longer linked to the destiny of the nation-state by virtue of its role as producer, protector, or inculcator of an idea of national culture. The process of economic globalization brings with it the relative decline of the nation-state as the prime instance of the reproduction of capital around the world. (p. 3)

Obviously, discourses on the meanings of universities within this scenario are strongly affected by the idea of becoming "key actors in the 'New Economy'" (Peters et al., 2009) where assumptions about knowledge and subjectivities are transformed to serve specific imaginings of the new present. Such ways to imagine universities under notions of economic globalization require discourses, practices, and people to put to work these assumptions. In this chapter, the focus is to understand how academics are becoming part of this way of reasoning universities. I contend that this happens as a complex web of institutional and cultural politics incites people to embody specific ideas about knowledge, institutional practices, and most importantly, about who they are, who they have been, and want to become.

To construct internationalization of higher education as related to discourses of competition, the nation, the market, has important effects on the configurations of knowledge, subjectivities, and their relations. Readings (1996) states that "the current crisis of the University of the West proceeds from a fundamental shift in its social role and internal systems, one which means that the centrality of the traditional humanistic disciplines to the life of the University is no longer assured" (p. 3). Interestingly, he develops the idea that universities were not always bureaucratic systems devoted to the pursuit of excellence, which he describes as the contemporary orientation of universities. Moreover, he explains that these shifts in the meanings of the university are associated to the loss of the nation-state as an elemental unit of capitalism. He further explains,

> ...since the nation-state is no longer the primary instance of the reproduction of global capital, "culture"—as the symbolic and political counterpart to the project of integration pursued by the nation-state—has lost its purchase. The nation-state and the modern notion of culture arose together, and they are [...] ceasing to be essential to an increasingly transnational global economy. (p. 12)

This way to imagine the university today has important implications for the manners in which we conceive subjectivities and practices at universities since, as this imagination acts as a unitary force to orient discourses and practices, it gains an unquestionable authority to guide desires and goals.

THE CASE OF LITERATURE

As institutional practices emphasize the importance of being recognized internationally, the use of the term knowledge in capitalist discourse, "has been limited in its scope and depth, that is, confined to understanding knowledge as an input and a good which enhances profitability" (Davidson-Harden, 2009, p. 271). Interesting to me is understanding how this use shapes writing practices and knowledge production. As has been noted, "...the talk of the knowledge economy represents, at its root, merely an extension or transformation of neoliberal capitalist discourse which works to deepen a perception of education seen through the lens of 'instrumental rationality'" (Davidson-Harden, 2009, p. 271). Specific ways to produce useful knowledge (for example, innovation or patenting) in this case represents a way to frame universities as tied to national competiveness and prosperity in which academics play a critical role.

For instance, in one interview with a male professor of Literature, I was interested in understanding the ways Literature as one key discipline in the crafting of national cultures and subjectivities was presented under these new requirements for universities. In other words, I was interested in how the popular idea that we are dealing with new forms of knowledge production, new practices of knowledge transferring, and new ways of building networks of relations between those who produce knowledge and its constitutive elements (Hohne and Schreck, 2009; Peters, 2009) were told by a professor in Literature. As we were talking, he was presenting his ideas about how curriculum (the formal way to understand knowledge) was one structural feature to respond to the demands of this new frame for universities. He explained his conception of knowledge and how he organized contents in his courses. The description he provides rests on the assumption that this is a new and innovative way of understanding and modeling knowledge in the field of Literature. He explains,

> ...we are going to prepare a program, at least structurally, that is similar to what astronauts use. As you train an astronaut you cannot teach him everything, if so the guy will shoot himself, he can't know everything about the spaceship and the universe, right? And if astronauts are taught this way, why I can't do the same with my first year students?

Knowledge seems not to connect to any specific content and is universally functional. By imagining knowledge this way, the object of the discipline is a matter of organization and distribution. This professor finds a way to "fit" into the new vision of what knowledge is and what are the purposes to produce it. To argue for the importance of the modularization of curriculum that provides a structural curricular organization to foster practices of homologization[2] worldwide, works as a way to align institutional discourses to the more global and institutional discourses of convergence. This impetus to standardize curriculum in order to render them comparable and calculable between institutions is a product of discourses of commodification of knowledge. "... by this very process, knowledge becomes a part of the structure of economic exchange, and its value is only acknowledged in terms of its status as an object of that exchange" (Hohne and Schreck, 2009, p. 499). As expected, this form of standardization affects the ways knowledge is thought, framed, and experienced; it also tells about practices of subjectivation associated to these notions of knowledge.

Then other questions come to the fore. If we rely on the idea developed by Readings (1996) that Literature is one of historical discipline where the constitution of national subjectivities and notions of culture are crafted, then how is "the national" and "culture" imagined today? As read from the interview excerpt presented above, it seems that organizing knowledge is becoming ever more indistinguishable from the mere production of a linear system of teaching and learning.

This way to speak of knowledge, as an economic exchange, has become a significant part of how this professor narrates what he does. In this orientation toward instrumentalization of knowledge, the acquisition and uses of knowledge become detached from knowledge itself, its meanings, its structures, and forms. This way to think knowledge implies an assimilation process of a certain order provided by the new discourses on what the university is. To equate teaching in universities with the management of content is a way to circulate ideas of knowledge as something, a positive object, and professors as active producers of these ideas. In this regard, Lyotard (1984) makes

an interesting contribution when declaring that this way of thinking knowledge (as compartments) is a way to disrupt knowledge as
narrative.

Later, the same professor explains, "operative knowledge is the
way the professor synthesizes knowledge for the student. In this way
[the student] does not relate to the total but parts of knowledge. It
does not imply superficiality but levels of depth...". Along with the
idea of knowledge itself, there is an explicit assumption about the
relationship between those who "deliver" and those who "receive"
knowledge, and it reinforces the imagination of knowledge as a form
of value. Lyotard (1984) explains, "knowledge is and will be produced in order to be sold, it is and will be consumed in order to be
valorized in a new production: in both cases, the goal is exchange.
Knowledge ceases to be an end in itself, it loses its "use-value" (p. 4).
The ways to narrate knowledge reproduces static relations between
content, teaching, and learning. Interestingly enough, these practices are presented as if they were new rules in the exercise of reasoning. These new ways of reasoning knowledge require a subject
to incarnate these assumptions (Readings, 1996) as they create new
cultural politics for universities. It fosters an unmarked subjectivity
for those who think knowledge.

Understanding knowledge as neutral and emphasizing the efficiency of its production closely relate to the affirmation of a neutral academic identity. As Grosz (1995) reminds us, "[knowledges]
do not simply *reflect* the social and historical contexts out of which
they were developed; rather, they help to actively inscribe or engender
the meaning of the social" (p. 43). As the professor from Literature
notes, the problem with knowledge becoming obsolete in the field of
Humanities has to do with "the problem of resistance to changes" he
shows us that the body is "an inscribed product of the intervention of
meanings" (Grosz, 1995, p. 39). More than assuming that academics reproduce dominant discourses (or resist them) this work complicates how academics relate to the social, cultural, and institutional
political directives to constitute themselves as knowledge producers.
Even though discourses of neutrality are powerful technologies to
craft selves, professors cannot embody the neutrality with which the
university presents itself, since academics are gendered and racially

marked. They are not universal subjectivities. Conversations with academics enable us to portray how the politics we think are located "out there" are lived through "in here," in our bodies, our minds, our everyday speech and practices.

With Whom I Work

In this section, I explore the ways in which the current pressures to publish on specific journals (ISI database) acts as technologies of reward and through them politics of subjectivation are enacted. I show how academic subjectivities are constituted as an effect of their relations to specific technologies of performance. The professors' incitement to be read as intelligible in contemporary academia, namely, being successful and recognized through specific academic experiences produces a "constitutive outside" (Butler, 1993, p. 188), a space that is imagined as unspeakable.

I use excerpts from female academics who work in one major university in Chile. This university was chosen because of its explicit effort to implement policies on internationalization. These two academics were interviewed to understand how their disciplinary trajectories may help configure the ways in which they, incited by discourses on efficiency and institutional reward, fight the logics of accountability and competitiveness as they are understood as natural ways for institutions to behave in present times. Some of the criteria to choose the participants were related to their interdisciplinary academic trajectories. It was also important that they had completed their graduate degrees abroad, and that they represent in some way those who do research out of the disciplinary mainstream. I intentionally sought descriptions of their academic work that may indicate some kind of interdisciplinarity or nontraditional orientation by reading their academic biographies and web descriptions of their scholarship. I also asked other professors for references of colleagues who may fit the profile required for these interviews. One of them comes from Theatre and her graduate studies were completed in Sociology. The other professor is from Aesthetics and her past degrees were in Literature and Philosophy. Their interviews have served to question my ideas about contemporary politics of writing. By politics of writing, I mean the exploration on how writing by women academics play itself out and in whose hands their success lies when making decisions about what to write and where to publish. When interviewing these women I wanted to understand how they narrate these processes through specific languages and intensities. I position the interview texts in the context of contemporary intellectual debates about market authority, blurred disciplinary boundaries, academic writing expectations, and the politics of knowledge production (Richardson, 2000) presented in the previous pages.

Here I am not interested in what academic writing might mean for specific disciplines or in particular contexts as I interviewed these women. Instead, I want to explore on the intensities of their experiences of writing as they fit within the more structural understandings of universities today. I want to understand where these intensities might go and what potential modes of orienting themselves and others (Stewart, 2007) are present in their narratives. One of my assumptions is that the ways women narrate experiences of writing provide the overarching frame of meaning for what goes on at the university. Studying academic narratives of practices of writing is a way to have access to the cultural politics of higher education institutions lived in actual bodies.

As presented in the interviews, questions about how knowledge is talked about and what are those mechanisms that participants use to narrate themselves are of interest. In doing this, my interests are oriented toward stressing the basic beliefs and assumptions the interviewees have in relation to writing and academic subjectivity, which are intrinsically related to their social and institutional effects. By exploring how academics narrate their institutional experiences I hope to understand how diverse discourses, specifically the statements related to regulation and monitoring, are deployed in the enactment of broader cultural academic practices. In many ways, this is an effort to link top-down and bottom-up discourses and practices of embodiment.

As I have mentioned throughout this chapter, writing as an activity is highly regulated by market mandates and reconfigures one's temporality. It forces the execution of particular strategies to perform as an academic. Writing, understood as a practice that privileges specific kinds of identities creates a "biopolitical economy of time" (Sharma, 2014, p. 138). This means that the institutional position one occupies because of the mantra of "productivity" is a result from where one fits. The experiences of women academics reveal how temporal and spatial inequities intensify when dominant ways of apprehending time and space guide normalizing discourses of success in universities. Writing as a space is not a container to be filled by academic activity. And it is because women's narratives and the ways they experience the act of writing that space cannot longer be understood as an a priori entity. One interesting feature of the interviews was the identification of writing as a masculine activity and it was expressed as those emotions that push women to question their ways to get closer or get separated from the act of writing. They use words such as frustration, desire, emulation, sacred, not brave enough, needed to be pushed to write, menace, anxiety, intuition, insecurity, lack of assertiveness, need to write otherwise, mystified, stained, marked, fear, authority, abandoning, and repression. All these words describe the meanings of writing to them. All these are ordinary affects to refer to the act of writing, but they make me question the intimate impact of the forces of circulation of discourses or normalized academic writing. As Katheleen Stewart (2007) proposes, affects "...are not so much forms of signification, or units of knowledge, as they are expressions of ideas or problems performed as a kind of involuntary and powerful learning and participation" (p. 40).

Another feature, and the reason I became fascinated by the narratives of these women, has to do with the distinction between the personal and the academic and how this distinction becomes blurred when they talk about the meanings of writing. When we were talking about the meanings of writing in academia today they went back to their childhood, to narrate stories of despair and pain. They reconstructed a narrative to tell the present of their politics of writing.

In other words, for these professors to communicate their politics of writing practices they have to access the everyday practices of space, time, and affect. I came to see the distinction when space, time, and affect are lived as abstractions, they "conveniently ignore [...] the ways in which differences of gender, age, class, 'race,' and the other forms of social differentiation shape people's lives" (Weems, 2010, p. 559). In the case of these women time, space, and affect became present, they were the instruments through which the complexity of what they were communicating was possible. Writing as time was expressed through the idea that cultural and institutional arrangements produce specific tempos for writing. This creates temporal inequities that intensify when dominant ways of apprehending time is guiding by discourses of productivity. As universities secure productivity, they secure a temporal order.

In what follows, I address the relationship between writing and power through the characterization of disciplines as spaces for specific productions of writing, affect as a possibility to narrate the material, and the masculine behind writing. The assumption behind this statement is that writing, as an affective activity expressed by these women is an act that resists disembodiment. Therefore, gender, as a performative attribute of subjects is also the product of spatial practices (Baydar, 2012). In other words, gender is an inseparable component of space.

THE MEANINGS OF WRITING

When women talk of the meanings of writing, we can interpret it as having textures. It is a physical activity, a moment of pleasure, an affective activity, a practice that causes conflicts and disturbs life in different ways. There is an ineffable connection between writing and reading as the participants manifest. The interviewee from Aesthetics expresses that "the more she reads the more she desires to write." She notes that because of this, writing is "imitation as well; it is a way to emulate the aesthetics of a book, to emulate the ways a writer describes something, the ways words take you to the place of imaginings."

She continues giving her reasons to write: "to me is to emulate the pleasure I got when I read. To write is a way of thinking. When you write you are active [it] is a way to remember." When reading these interviews with women I came to understand that the intimacy of writing functions as a political technology. As Richardson (2000) explains, "We are always present in our texts, no matter how we try to suppress ourselves. We are always writing in particular contexts-contexts that affect what and how we write and who we become. Power relations are always present" (p. 154). As I move through the interviews, the participants expressed how writing belongs to specific ways to frame time. This professor noted that she feels she "writ[es] the entire day." She feels that writing is a permanent activity that does not belong to a specific place and time. Writing then, becomes a way of manifesting an intellectual act for her. The temporal sense of writing shows up.

SPACE AND POLITICS

As I was moving through the ways these women were telling themselves I was interested in the political positions their writing activities had, institutionally speaking. I became interested in how the production of institutional space was constitutive of the meanings to writing practices they were producing. For instance, the professor from Theater describes her way to develop her work during the Dictatorship period in Chile,

> ...well, [...] we created [this] center for cultural experimentation and it was founded by 80% of my colleagues at the university. We found this center in parallel [to those activities at the university]. We started this critical intellectual organic movement with the purpose to diagnose [cultural and social] contexts. We wanted to locate those new artistic creative movements under this new political situation [the Dictatorship]. We wanted to know about the cultural and structural transformations of the country, about the effects of the limits of freedom of speech, the re-structuration of academic languages, the new relationships with audiences [...]. Finally, how alternative discursive grids in the fields of Arts were constituted.

Later, she describes how she lived this political spatial duality to be able to express her and her colleagues' academic and political interests,

> [in this center] we produced research that we were not allowed to develop at the university because of the political situation. Imagine we were the same people, here and there [the university and the center]. Do you see what I am saying? So, we defined those research questions possible to be answered at the university and those possible for the center. We distributed the political dimensions of our work [laughing] in relation to the institutional space. I think you never stop doing politics when talking of either Arts or knowledge.

Several issues are interesting in this way of framing the production of knowledge. The political aspect of what she does and how she narrates space understood as coherent to the political demands becomes important in her way to define what she does. A body marked by political and institutional facts is the background from where she defines herself as a professor. Her body expresses "the relationship between forces" (Olkowski, 1999, p. 98) and through her narrative, I recognize that the relations between those forces are not constructed outside of the body.

As it pertains to gender, representations of knowledge as neutral and as a matter of organization, is an efficient way to divert the political dimension of bodies in the production of knowledge. To liberate the body from what it does (writing) justifies the required and desirable neutrality when writing. As I move through these women's interviews I see the operations of the body as central to understand the politics of today's practices of reward and legitimation in universities. As Grosz (1995) reminds us, "[knowledges] do not simply *reflect* the social and historical contexts out of which they were developed; rather, they help to actively inscribe or engender the meaning of the social" (p. 43).

Knowledges are the products of sexually specific bodies (Grosz, 1995, p.41) located in specific spaces and times, a relation that neoliberal thinking intends to overshadow. Differences in what the participants choose to tell about their academic trajectories tell about the particular densities and intensities in connecting bodies to knowledges. Consider for instance, when the participants narrate their political experience when dealing with issues of publishing at the university. They refer to the restrictions within the fields of Humanities and Social Sciences to publish. The Theater professor explains,

> ...I feel that the field of Humanities should have the freedom to propose genres, to propose the ways to perform this reflexive work because it has different logics, just because it is a different way to organize knowledge. Creative work goes for a different track and society also needs another way to frame knowledge. Look, what I say is that a scientific journal is going to be read by scientists in order to understand the complexities of any specific topic. They belong to a [very specific]

discipline, but Arts is not that, Arts talks about the human being, about the construction of subjectivities, about processing contemporary issues, about experience, ways of living, about social relations, about power. These are issues concerning anyone. Therefore, what it is produced in here it is something to feed the national collective imaginary. [Not to pay attention to this way of producing knowledge] is to cut the flows between the university and society.

Later, she tells the story of being an editor of a journal in the College of Arts,

I was the head [of the journal] for 25 years. The cultural capital that this initiative created was wonderful, I feel it is a long-life connection. But the fact that the college now has to index the journal has meant that all those journal sections that I really loved are gone. For instance, that section named 'words from those who create' is going to disappear.

She further expresses,

…mainstream academic culture imposes itself aggressively on academics and the artists who were used to publishing in the journal feel that they do not have the tools to respond to these requirements. So, many of them are now publishing in other places. They feel that the ISI exigency level does not correspond to their ways of expressing their work. Mostly, because it restructures the way they organize their thinking. Thus, it is not that they do not have an interesting thinking structure or valuable hypotheses. Rather, the ways they structure knowledge are different, particularly the ways to communicate artistic knowledge. We all know that academic mainstream culture has a model and that there are people ready to apply it and that the productivity level is high. But in this case, we are a little displaced and I feel that the way to generate knowledge in the field of Arts and Humanities is a different one. More than anything, I value a profound conversation with an artist.

Then, the effects of these ways to frame circuits of recognition and reward in universities are oriented to identify and characterize subjectivities producing particular ideas of what knowledge is and what the effects of specific politics of subjectivation are. But, overall the production of critically different academic spaces to produce academic writing operates through the informal production of regularities (Massumi, 2002). Besides being widely promoted by the institutional culture of the entrepreneurial academic subjectivity and the rewarding system, academics themselves produce and circulate regularities when describing what it means to write. What I argue is that gender and the ways these women talk about the experience of writing shows the invisible power of these regularities when thinking about the possible writing. With no doubt the discourses of the *useful* knowledge have come to transform institutional spaces used by academics. What I want to show is how the already-constituted relations of gender (meaning patriarchy and subordination) operate in these women's narratives to explain what they do and who they are in academia. As Massumi (2002) tells, "The modeling occurs through the accumulation of already-constituted relations, contracted into bodies as habits (which includes belief: habituated meaning)" (p. 82).

Even though it is easier to recognize that the conversation about cultural politics is much conceived as a threat in the Humanities and Social Sciences than in hard Sciences in universities, I do not want to follow the traditional argument that Humanities and Social Sciences are the essence of the university in terms of cultural politics. In fact, by analyzing narratives on how writing is thought by these academics I realize that those attributes belonging to the natural or hard sciences as without politics have moved to other spheres of academic work. When talking about how academics construct knowledge and the discourses and resources they use, I see the institutionalization of neutral politics of knowledge that guards specific subjectivities and relations.

THE SPACE OF WRITING

As I move through the interview texts, the spatializing dimension of writing takes place. The professor of Aesthetics describes the ways women approached the act of writing at the beginning of the twentieth century. She described it as "an essentially intimate act, it was through the writing of letters that the world of writing was possible for women. It was a private world it was not a public discourse for women." I wonder in what ways a specific kind of writing continues being a private and intimate act. The ways women describe those fears related to do "the real" writing, the kind of writing that they really desire to produce, suggests that the private as a space for women to write has not disappeared. To become a public writer in academia today one has to follow the parameters that indicate what is worth writing. This is different from what these women are naming as "the real writing" for them.

The same professor states, "I love writing but the kind of writing that I desire the most I do not dare to do it." She also notes that "I need someone to push me to write." On the same topic, the other professor from Theater expresses, "I always felt that knowledge, that creative moment of production was always on the other person. Then, my status or position when writing was to cheer up, provoke, motivate, organize in some ways the other's thinking." In following the idea of regularities presented by Massumi (2012) to fear and stay behind the creative person are ways to reproduce a very specific understanding of women in the space of writing. To be produced as the Other in the space of writing requires emotions of despair and rejection to operate. How are these emotions produced in women's narrations in relation to writing? How is it that writing becomes a site of struggle for women? These fears, or the need to be behind the person who "really" has something to say, parallels with what Irigaray (as cited in Baydar, 2012) has listed as "the masculine uses of languages, principles of identity, non-contradiction and binarisms" (p. 701). The ways these "attributes" orient those decisions professors made to be part of the circuits of privilege serve specific relations of power, hierarchy, and exclusion.

To understand the effects of these emotions, the professor of Theater explains, "I have never known if one makes the inhabited place and that it has its own limits, or if I have to go to those places that better suit me." This sentence shows how the idea of space operates to allow a political understanding of herself and what she does in academia. Space as limited and restricted permits few and recognized political options to be possible. It is not surprising that such ways of imagining themselves as academics presents the contradictions of the meanings of institutional practices. The "new" academic subjectivities proliferated by discourses of the entrepreneurial university incite the possibility of a revitalized academic identity as something of a second nature that contains all predetermined characteristics of something given. Professors have to make smart choices in creating academic trajectories. It is a way to develop a personal strategy and take personal responsibility for their success by making right choices in this competitive environment.

WRITING SCENES

As I move through the conversations with these professors different ways of writing depending on the discipline are presented. Journalism, Aesthetics, and Philosophy are presented as critical examples to show differences on how to approach the self through writing in a specific disciplinary field. Aesthetics, for instance, is felt as a place where the interviewee felt freer to write. For her it was *the* "space of critique." She says, "It was not like being in the space of total freedom and experiencing a sacred activity," as she refers to writing in the field of Literature, "but it was a better place than Journalism." Disciplines are experienced as places embedded with certain practices and ways to understand oneself as a writer desiring or repressing oneself. These places have their own "intellectual tics." These "tics" refer to the ways power shifts. As Bronwyn Davies (2000) mentions, "Depending on the discipline the subject is positioned by and within multiple competing discourses they encounter, they can begin to imagine how to reposition themselves, realign themselves, and use the power of discourse they have to disrupt those or its effects they wish to resist (p. 180). Writing, then, is seen as a question of competence in specific disciplines. For instance, she notes that her experience writing in Philosophy (while completing her doctorate) was a time of a constant anxiety. This was mainly because she wanted to position herself in order to expose her politics in her research problem. As she moved through the impossibility to locate her fear and impossibility to write she experienced the political power of being silent in academia. As Richardson (2000) notes, "Social scientific disciplines' story line includes telling writers to suppress their own voices, adopt the all-knowing, all-powerful voice of the academy, and keep their mouths shut about academic in-house politics" (p. 154). In the case of this professor and the ways she narrates how she lives and experiences writing, I can tell that her life is tied to the disciplines and the chances she has to face the power of the discipline itself. In many ways, her ability to construct herself as a writer depends on how she is able to unravel the privilege of disciplines. When she was telling differences in writing in Philosophy, she recognizes the power in this field. Here "[the]'masculine' describes not a biological category but a cognitive style, an epistemological stance. Its key term is detachment: from the emotional life, from the particularities of time and place, from personal quirks, prejudices, and interests, and most centrally from the object itself" (Bordo, 1986, p. 451).

If we wish to write, attention to places is required. To practice the space of Philosophy or to practice the space of Journalism, requires a political understanding of the meanings of writing. And this has an effect on the ways "disciplines classify propositions either as 'their own' or as 'outside' their disciplinary boundaries [this] is a political and not simply an intellectual matter" (Grosz, 1995, p. 232).

There is a way to interpret "academic writing" as implying that the one who writes is universal and uniform. The ways in which writing is organized—as mechanic and providing a linear account of the procedures and results of a research study—implies an idea of academia as a particular space. However, the descriptions of the meanings of writing of these two women are inscribed with different modes of sexuality, race, class, and so on. I argue that it is important to understand the ways hegemonic ideas about writing from specific bodies and within specific fields are lived by ourselves.

AFFECT AND WRITING. THE INVISIBLE AUTHORITY

As I read the interviews with these women, other intensities showed up. The professor of Aesthetics tells me, "I need to move from a frustrated and frightened relation to writing to a different one. This has been a relation where I see the same authoritarian experiences that you can see in your personal life." Whenever you write you feel that there is someone on your back watching over your thoughts, your tones, the ways you experiment with textual forms, with content, with voice, with frames. Writing means dealing with that invisible authority.

She continues her story, "[because of the pleasure she gets from reading and writing,] I suffered a lot at home when I was a child. And I think it was because I was a woman. Once I remember I was walking with my father along the street and he looked at a little girl who was sweeping a front yard. He looked at me and said 'this is exactly what you should be doing, you should behave like this little girl'." Then, she continues, "For this same reason I feel insecure when writing. It is hard to explain the feeling. I get confused, I criticize myself a lot, and suffer. I want to write something then I decide not to, I regret, and at the end I got a lot of paragraphs. In fact, I define myself as a paragraphs writer." No doubt that writing for this professor is imbricated with life. To understand your own politics of writing, you have to cut certain ties, dependencies, and repressions in order to have a more fluid relation, a more authorized, quieter and less anxious relation to writing. As Patricia Ticineto Clough with Jean Halley (2007, p.2) note "...language only captures what has emerged from the level of intensity, [therefore] affect cannot be exposed through language" (p.192). Therefore, what I get from these interviews "...are not representations of what has happened in affect, but, rather, indications of the significance for the organism or system of what has happened in affect" (Clough and Halley, 2007, p. 193). Thus, attention needs to be focused on "meaning" as the participants indicate.

To be affected was translated into the idea that "I need to write in a different way." In another line she says, "I have always felt afraid of that kind of writing that gives you more freedom, more creative." She also refers to writing as a physical activity,

> Once, my mother wanted to throw all my books because she said that they were the cause of my allergies and asthma. My world of reading and writing has always been threatened. My parents have always tried to change my world. Once my dad gave me a guitar, he wanted me to learn how to play the guitar. He thought that switching to playing an instrument instead of reading will make me happier. He thought I was always depressed because of reading.

Here writing, being a woman, and an adolescent are intersecting ways to talk about pleasure. Pleasure seems to be intelligible only when it is performed "within reason" (McWilliam, 2000, p. 164) and specific emotions orient life to be lived as "good lives." In here, authorities over writing were used as "technolog[ies] or instrument[s] which allow[...] the reorientation of individual desire toward a common goal" (Ahmed, 2010, p. 59).

In different ways, both interviewees resist the intellectualization of affects since affect is vital to their ways of announcing meanings of writing. However, they nonetheless note that the affective realm of writing is from where they begin to think bigger things. As McWilliam (2000) notes "Put simply, the end is to constantly unsettle what it means for women to behave properly in the academy—and to take pleasure in doing it" (p. 176).

MISTY THOUGHTS

Moving through the texts created with these women, I have come to understand that notions of space and time are critical for theorizing about the cultural politics of writing for women today. Academics' narratives show how they embody the invisible forces that give shape to individual behaviors through institutional practices and market forces. Academics' practices show how their academic lives have become governed "through the university" and through a social norm where their bodies, experiences, and academic lives take shape and meaning. Through this way of embodying meanings, antagonistic spaces are created and consequent regulatory practices installed. Invisible systems of monitoring, regulation, and control constitute themselves as a regime of truth about what is read as academic work. Such systems codify and disseminate information about "normal experiences" in academia.

In many ways the exploration of academics' narratives is an account of the productive possibilities offered by the articulations of neoliberal governance in universities. This is particularly relevant when the interest is focused on the extent to which neoliberal discourses are embodied by individual policymakers, academics, and higher education administrators. It is through academics' narratives that I explore other signs that show that what is in place is a reproduction of hierarchies that are situated in discourses of academic success and assumptions of neutral academic discourse.

The purpose of this chapter has been to illustrate and question dominant ways of talking about writing in academia without trying to replace them with others. Instead, it has been my attempt at revealing the contemporary *politics* of reasoning women's practices and discourses in academia.

DISSOLVING

One of the major purposes of this book has been to dissolve dominant notions of time and space when looked at through the experiences of *bodies in motion*. In these pages I have shown how current discourses of internationalization of higher education have emerged as an institutional force that allows for other discourses to proliferate. I have presented stories of international graduate students and male and female professors who have completed their degrees somewhere outside of Chile to show the workings of particular ways to produce international subjectivities in institutional spaces. All these stories have something in common: they are possibilities for me to question the ways time and space in their dominant conceptualizations shape our understandings of who we are in academia. These productions are being framed by aggressive policies on higher education that present internationalization discourses and practices as the ways universities align themselves with market's requirements. An examination of discourses generated within official documents and research studies has also been included in this book. They have provided specific understandings about the ways discourses of the immigrant, the strange, or the student as a threat take shape and gain authority within the discursive web of international initiatives.

Throughout the writing of this book, I suggest that more complicated conceptualizations of time and space are required because they can eventually give us a different perspective on issues presented by the participants. Dominant notions of nation, progress, knowledge, and subjectivities are contested throughout the book. For instance, one of the interesting features to pay attention to when revisiting the interviews used in this book is how the exclusionary narrative of the nation is used in internationalization discourses. The concept of nation has an effect on the ways politics of exclusion are put to work in higher education institutions. Its languages and practices structure institutions to produce clear distinctions between "qualified and unqualified bodies" (Manning, 2003, p. xv) through explicit policies and implicit actions. The people presented in the seven chapters that complete this book talk about (albeit not without ambivalence) the meanings of feeling attached and obey the "natural" and fictitious correspondences between territories and identities. In different registers this correspondence acts as an invisible power that orients desires, expectations, and purposes for the interviewees. This relation, based on the assumption that space is something people fill in and time something people can cut out and segment to narrate oneself, is productive in such a way that it maintains essentialist discourses of the Other. I wonder what is at stake when this relation of territory and identity is uncovered. What are the political effects when dismantling the strict correspondence between belonging and geography, and what consequences may arise as a result of the ways we understand knowledge and subjectivities in higher education today. In different chapters I have shown how the power of the language of the nation generates discourses of exclusion and disqualification and justifies particular policies in higher education institutions today.

Along with the problematization of the languages of the nation, the power of dominant concepts of space and time also give life to other productions. For instance, home and nostalgia allow the understanding of complexities of the geopolitics of intellectual practices in the context of internationalization of higher education. Nostalgia as a productive practice authorizes linear conceptualizations of time and contained experiences of space. Nostalgia as a force distributes power around specific articulations between the subject and territory. It shapes narratives of movement and locates experiences in segments of memory. Past stories have a different tone and intensity when describing the present and this is because of nostalgic impulses. Nostalgic past stories become the underlying structure to produce a particular future. As it is, nostalgia serves institutional purposes very well. It incites people to perform (without too much questioning or resistance) particular and limited nationalities (a Japanese woman performs Japan, a Kenyan man performs Kenya, a Chilean woman performs Chile). This political distribution of international bodies in higher education institutions facilitates the workings of regulation and monitoring.

Participants of this work show how the power of dominant notions of time and space travel through specific ways to name experiences of movement. The restricted and limited registers with which they give life to their narrations (the "foreigner," "the stranger," "home," "away," and so on) speak of a way to frame life that is based on particular imaginings of space and time. The vocabulary of space as a container and time as fragmentation underlie their stories.

As "a path is not composed of positions" (Massumi, 2002, p. 6) to believe that the stories told by the participants of this book are unitary and reflect a singular unity of movement would be naïve. As they move within their memories of places and past times they also describe a space of potential becoming. Whenever you look at the middle of their stories, in the threads of the becoming of a narrative, something else is being said. The usual way to read the interviews would be as divisible stories that frame a particular meaning. Instead, when the reader intends to look beyond this fictional unity to produce meaning there is a constant drifting, a flexible oscillation of possibilities for understanding something different.

Each of the seven chapters that comprise this book, accomplishes specific purposes to show distinctive themes as part of the trajectories experienced by graduate international students and faculty. The blending of the seven chapters creates a stimulating path through pasts, presents, and futures, as well as different geographies and landscapes. Through the different stories I use Chile and the United States as points of reference and as metaphors when discussing issues of time and space in relation to how knowledge, genders, and practices are constructed under the framework of internationalization of higher education. The critical articulations of the self in relation to time and space under institutional discourses of internationalization provide a rich context to destabilize current subjectivities and other concepts of movement, borders, and flux, as presented as characteristics of the global age.

My purpose throughout this book has been not only to understand how bodies in motion are transformed by the experience of movement but also to engage in an interrogation of the discursive and disciplinary forms that take shape under dominant discourses of space and time that are strategically embedded in higher educational policies. The stories and people's experiences presented serve this purpose as they are subjects positioned in a range of contradictory places that co-exist. Hopefully, these narratives will offer new perspectives on the constraints and possibilities for the future of policymaking and research regarding internationalization of higher education and the potential for knowledge and identities production.

As I have stated earlier, the assumptions and purposes I bring to this project are clearly affected by my own trajectory between geographies, languages, and disciplines. I am able to locate my own spatial and temporal narratives as important sites to produce accounts of personal lives. Throughout the chapters I have presented my theoretical, practical, epistemological, and methodological reflections with the intention to disrupt and interrogate dominant conceptualizations of space and time and their effect of producing static notions of people, ideas of desirable homogeneity, and what happens when they are portrayed in policies and university documents. This messy process has enabled me to raise new concerns, questions, and thoughts that interrogate the usual ways we overlook time and space in the construction of who we are.

To show international faculty stories of movement and to speak of the complexities of their travel is a perfect scenario to question the idea of the essential self as an obvious representation. To focus attention on movement and transition when speaking about the subject means that she/he will barely coincide with those ideas that we usually use to secure the meaning of our stories: home, territory, nation, and culture. They seem to lose their appealing essence when describing these people's experiences of movement. When I turn the lens toward how variations and inconsistencies are constitutive part of these people's narratives something opens up; a possibility to expand the political arguments about the meanings of moving in academic today. Then, I ask myself what would happen to the ways we qualify experiences of movement today, what if instead of insisting on fixity we pay attention to variation and transitions of people's narratives? How would this understanding affect policymaking and research about international movement within academia? If policies and research create subjects to be regulated then both researchers and policymakers need to be aware of this fundamental but troubling understanding of the self. If there is not a real definite subject then what is the intellectual exercise that needs to be done in order to address this new fragmented subject? I would argue that it has to do with the constant variation of the subject, in the diffusion of the boundaries of what it means to be a complete and unified subject that research and policymakers need to look at and rethink their research questions and regulations. The conceptualizations of time and space we use to make sense of the world we inhabit are constitutive of the kinds of questions we create about others and ourselves.

How do I know that the subject has been disrupted from her/his static position? I think that because the processes the subject has engaged in to create a space for critiquing those elements that give her/him stability to life, the subject enters a process of developing a new sense of self. Processes such as movement remove international academics from stable communities that provide them with a sense of discontinuity between their "original" place and intellectual activity. The result is that they feel themselves becoming fractured as they run different ways; and at each place they encounter different sets of values and expectations of them. The resulting loss of a stable identity ends up as a questioning of the truths they hold about themselves and the world they inhabit. For some people, this brings a scenario of uncertainty, insecurity, and anxiety. For others this is the way subjects exist everywhere, in a constant, unending process of becoming, a constant recreation of who they were, and imagining who they will become. Flux and change have become usual for them and the seduction of being in different places has flourished. This sense of constantly being in flux and challenging the fixity of reality (in its modernistic fashion) brings change and transforms their sense of identity.

These dynamics of movement and flux underlying the texts presented in the previous chapters lead me to begin questioning truth itself, not only truth about ourselves but also the truth about the world we live in. There is no one *story*, which explains everything. So, the truth provided by policies and research about international movement should be contested because it purports to give finite answers for the nature of this community and the world around them. I emphasize that as policies and research construct truths about the subjects they regulate, often obscuring all individual stories, discourses themselves lack complexities and tensions. The case of NAFSA[1] represents an example on how within and between institutions different discourses and contradictory positions about international faculty may be sustained. For instance, discourses pronounced by policies about international students examined in this study present specific identities to be worn by international students in the United States As such, expectations and limits for what international students can and cannot do are defined. And, since this represents a hegemonic power relation, it is imperative to be suspicious of what policies say and in what ways they are used as tools for producing and circulating particular ideas of the international body, of nations, and relations between them.

What does this mean for the international academic community? It means that policies create an image of the international faculty that constitutes public knowledge, thereby creating a restricted and limited context around them and reinstalling the operations of a fixed and unflexible matrix on which to locate people. The problem is that this collective knowledge is charged with ideology. To make a person a subject to be regulated is to impose on that person certain limits, regulating in this way the availability of experiences. This impedes the expression of the multidimensionality of subjects' lives and does not recognize that we are constantly in the process of becoming with many different, and often incongruent, identities existing simultaneously and overlapping in significant ways.

What the participants' stories in this research have represented is the image of a subject who is constantly questioning those discourses that give life to them. I see this process as a manifestation of the idea that the self is constantly redefined and that identity constantly undergoes change. This constant transition, as a constitutive characteristic of people's lives, is political in such a way that restructures the notions of the subject of research and the subject of policy. To change the idea of the subject of research from definite to fragmented implies to adjust the ways we frame basic questions of what we do. How can we grasp the variation of the subject in research and policies? If subjects are the effect of the question (Colebrook, 1999), then what are the kinds of questions to be asked? What should be the notions of time and space operating behind the ways we ask questions about the subject? To properly address these questions we need to look at how the spaces we live in and the ways we recall pasts and foresee future moments are constructed. And this is what the participants in this book have shown us. To narrate their experiences as intellectuals in a country not their own is a way to address the complexities of the experience of time and space.

I have come to understand that policies and research reflect the old idea that the goal of the subject should be to achieve wholeness, to find the integrated self, to pull all the seemingly different parts of ourselves together into one cohesive and coherent whole. In contrast, what I have argued in these chapters is that this cohesive and coherent whole cannot happen when we pay attention to individual narratives of international movement subjects. They cannot become one cohesive self. It is more like they are constantly struggling with the idea of fitting into the languages of fixity, boundary, territory, belonging, and correspondence. By paying attention to what exceed these languages in the participants' narratives, I can see there is a potential to transform the usual understandings of the experiences of movement. Something new may happen; a new subject can be imagined.

What operates behind the narratives and texts I have presented is the belief that identity is a way to gather people together around one dimension and that secure rights for them. But, identity can constitute a fundamental element to discuss the operations of power when issues of difference appear. I have shown the constraining nature of official documents and research about international bodies and those stories narrated by international people themselves. This has led me to think of what ideas lie behind these ways to frame international experiences of movement as time and space come to the fore.

SPACE IS ONLY RHYTHM. TIME IS JUST AIR

The writing of this book has been an experience in itself. Experience in the sense that I have been questioning my own perpetual unflexible grids in order to write what I want to say. In many ways, this has been a work of confrontation of truths about the ways people should live their lives and the incongruences that are evident when these truths do not come up easily or as natural, or as expected. To present tensions between the powerful forces telling who international faculty and students are and their stories was my way of connecting possibilities of producing institutional subjectivities, times to be lived in, and spaces described as neutral and passive containers. Hopefully, the conversation around the effects of unquestionable usage of dominant notions of time and space will bring forward a conversation on the conditions of emergence, contestation, and transformation of the meanings and form of discourses of international movement.

An interesting and revealing part of this journey has been to understand how the participants contest the research and policy discourses imposed on them. I believe that it is important to reveal why international faculty and students' representations have been silent and only addressed by marginalization and compensatory discourses. Some questions that populated my mind while writing this book were: why have faculty and international students been coopted by the rhetoric of internationalization of education? Why, if the constitution of the universities is greatly international, is there a such a limited representation of international movement with all its complexities?

To answer these questions I had to go back to some of my initial ideas around this work. It depends on where I am and how I am perceived, prescribed, named, and authorized to be. This brings unexpected elements to which to attend for countries interested in becoming important centers for recruiting international faculty for the future. This is why I think it is important to ask questions about the ways they inhabit places and how they interpret pasts, presents, and futures. Identities are shaped by embodied and embedded narratives located in particular places. A space and a time become *something* by being invested with meaning, a social signification that produces identity, by being named. Time becomes a way to structure personal stories. The presumed certainties of cultural identity, firmly located in particular places and times that sustain stable communities, are disputed and displaced by international students and faculty's practices.

In relation to movement, what seems relevant is that international students and faculty accomplish a journey that has two dimensions. First, their journey has a material dimension where travel implies movement between fixed positions: from one country to another. But, because of the predictability of this dimension of the journey, there is knowledge about the places and, more importantly, there are expectations associated with these places. The second dimension is a more imaginary travel and it becomes a more critical activity. In this more imaginary travel, there are no points of departure or arrival. This ghostly journey represents all the aspirations and well-intentioned visions of their subjectivities in a more cosmopolitan world. The uncertainty of this dimension of international students' and faculty travel is what shapes the notion of becoming an intellectual *in motion*. Because of the lack of research in this line, ways of producing knowledge have not been addressed properly. There has been a loss in terms of theorization of new logics of production and dissemination of knowledge. As Lawrence Grossberg (2000) states, "instead we must embrace temporality in the celebration of imagination, as the attempt to discover new ways of belonging to time, to the past as well as to the present and the future. In this way we might also begin to imagine new forms and formation of a political will, and political collectivities capable of imagining new futures" (p. 159).

The multiple positions occupied by international students and faculty have not received significant attention because they have been regarded as integrated in other groups' interests or concerns, or simply erased through the rhetoric of massive movements around the world. I strongly believe that the multiple positions imagined by international faculty and students are important because they constitute a context for theorizing new dynamics of knowledge creation. They are not static subjects mobilizing culture, they are not people in need of remediation, nor are they cultural ambassadors. Instead, they are critical intellectuals imagining a place in the world for them where to create and recreate knowledge differently. Because of their experiences, they feel the need to become part of the world and existing discourses have been acting as limits for these imaginaries. The multiple positionality of international faculty and students has not been theorized in consideration with the specificities of this new globalized condition. I say new condition because I think that international students have been theorized in a very static way, and I am arguing that to better represent these subjects, one needs to look at the more general context of globalization to make sure to understand where this subject is imagining her/himself. To continue reading research and policies about international academics in a negative and assimilationist way does not help to attain a more expanded and deconstructive understanding of subjectivity and movement limiting dangerously the possible imaginations about this group of people.

International faculty and students are important because they become a specific type of intellectual who challenge static processes of appropriation, expatriation, and hybridization of knowledge. Subsequent interrogations would include, what does it mean at the beginning of the twentieth-first century to speak of the international faculty as an intellectual in motion? What are the possibilities for conceiving this intellectual? What type of knowledge may be created? What is the role of universities in this understanding of interconnected, nonstatic production of knowledge and subjectivity? What does it mean to write as an intellectual in a different language, and challenge the personal assumptions about reality and research?

Separated from their supposedly *authentic* place, international faculty start an ontological travel around what they do. The passive belonging to specific places becomes radically denaturalized because of the complexity of the intellectual, social, and cultural processes they undergo. I believe that there is a need to facilitate a practice of wandering for international faculty. For instance, there is no research on what kind of knowledges, and theories international students produce. I believe it is necessary to think that if intellectuals are traveling around the world, then they theorize from somewhere else. Travel then becomes a political practice where the subject is able to imagine more easily and be aware of her/his fragmentation processes. I think that movements and practices created by international faculty imply intellectual creation connected to deconstructive readings of places they inhabit and their subjectivities.

Finally, I have been arguing throughout this book that monolithic categories of international faculty and students obscure relevant stories and processes lived and created by them. Deconstructing discourses generated by policies and research on international people requires imagining notions of space and time in different configurations. In the age of the celebration of the disordering of subjectivities, policies and research need to reflect these changes, and universities need to become the loci for rethinking the political function of movement in the present times of globalization. I believe there is a need to consider new ways to talk about the temporalities of concepts, the truths about the places we inhabit, the new ways of belonging, and the new ways of speaking about time for subjects. This is what I have sought to do in this book: to make visible the political dimension necessary to push ourselves to think otherwise.

Notes

Introduction Times and Spaces of Concepts

1. See also Eugenie Brinkema (2012). A mother is a form of time: *Gilmore Girls* and the elasticity of in-finitude. *Discourse* 34(1), pp. 3–31.
2. See C. Matus and S. Talburt (2013). Producing global citizens for the future: space, discourse, and curricular reform. *Compare: A Journal of Comparative and International Education*, 45(2), pp. 226–247.
3. See also Erica Levin (2011). Affect in the age of neoliberalism. *Discourse*, 33(2), pp. 280–283; Jeff Pruchnic (2008). The invisible gland: affect ad political economy. *Criticism*, 50(1), pp. 160–175; C. Matus and M. Infante (2011). Undoing diversity: knowledge and neoliberal discourses in colleges of education. *Discourse: Studies in Cultural Politics of Education*, 32(3), pp. 293–307.
4. See also Claudia Matus and Susan Talburt (2009). Spatial Imaginaries: universities, internationalization, and feminist geographies. *Discourse: Studies in the Cultural Politics of Education*, 30(4), pp. 515–527.
5. Liz Bondi (2005). Making connections and thinking through emotions: between geography and psychotherapy. *Transactions of the Institute of British Georgraphers*, 30, pp. 433–448; Nhi Lieu (2008) Toward a "subjectless" discourse: engaging transnationalist and postcolonial approaches in Asian American Studies. *American Quarterly*, 60(2), pp. 491–496; Jasbir Puar (2002). Circuits of Queer mobility: Tourism, travel, and globalization. *GLQ: A Journal of Lesbian and Gay Studies*, 8(1–2), pp. 101–137.

6. See more on this discussion in Fazal Rizvi (2003). *Identities on the move: student mobility and the uses of international education.* In S. Yoong (ed.) *Globalization and Multicultural Perspectivesin Education.* Penang: Universiti Sains Malaysia Press.

7. Open Door Reports are provided by the Institute of International Education (IIE), which focuses on International Student Exchange and Aid, Foreign Affairs, and International Peace and Security.

8. IDP Australia is an international educational organization offering student placement in Australia and other countries.

9. See Fazal Rizvi (2012). *Mobilities and the transnationalization of youth cultures.* In Nancy Lesko and Susan Talburt (eds.) *Keywords in Youth Studies. Tracing Affects, Movements, Knowledges.* New York and London: Routledge, pp. 191–203; Fazal Rizvi and Bob Lingard (2010). *Globalizing Education Policy.* London and New York: Routledge.

10. See also John Evans (2014). *Ideational border crossings: rethinking the politics of knowledge within and across disciplines. Discourse: Studies in the Cultural Politics of Education,* 35(1), pp. 45–60.

11. See also James Paul Gee (2005). *An Introduction to Discourse Analysis. Theory and Method.* New York: Routledge; James Paul Gee and Michael Handford (eds.) (2014). *The Routledge Handbook of Discourse Analysis.* London and New York: Routledge; Ruth Wodak and Michael Meyer (eds.) (2009). *Methods of Critical Discourse Analysis.* Thousand Oaks: Sage; Margaret Wetherell, Stephanie Taylor, and Simeon J. Yates (2010). *Discourse Theory and Practice. A Reader.* Thousand Oaks: Sage.

1   METHODOLOGICAL TWISTS AND THEORETICAL TOOLS

1. To explore on similar ways to conceptualize space see Liz Bondi (2005). *Gender and the Reality of Cities: embodies identities, social relations and performativities,* on line papers archived by the *Institute of Geography. School of Geosciences,*

University of Edinburgh; Larry Knopp (2004). Ontologies of place, placelessness, and movement: queer quests for identity and their impacts on contemporary geographic thought. *Gender, Space & Culture*, 11(1), pp. 121–134; Claude Raffestin (2002). Space, territory, and territoriality. *Environment and Planning D: Society and Space*, 30, pp. 121–141.

2. See the discussion on flexibility in thinking different stages of research: Emily Billo and Nancy Hiemstra (2013). Mediating messiness: expanding ideas of flexibility, reflexibity, and embodiment in fieldwork. *Gender, Place & Culture: A Journal of Feminist Geography*, 20(3), 313–328.

3. See Carey-Ann Morrison (2010). Heterosexuality and home: Intimacies of space and spaces of touch. *Emotion, Space and Society*, xxx, pp. 1–9.

4. See also other discussions on how to research human space: Denise Bijoux and Jameson Myers (2006). Interviews, solicited Diaries and photography: "new" ways of accessing everyday experiences of place. *Graduate Journal of Asian-Pacific Studies*, 4:1, pp. 44–64; Deborah Britzman (1997). On refusing explication: towards a non-narrative narrativity. *Resources for Feminist Research*, 25, pp. 3–13; Alan Latham (2003). Research, performance, and doing human geography: some reflections on the diary-photograph, diary-interview method. *Environment and Planning A*, 35, pp. 1993–2017.

5. See Matt Baillie Smith and Katy Jenkins (2012). Editorial, emotional methodologies-the emotional spaces of International Development. *Emotion, Space and Society*, 5, pp. 75–77.

6. See also Alison Rooke (2009). Queer in the field: on emotions, temporality, and performativity in Ethnography. *Journal of Lesbian Studies*, 13(2), pp. 149–160; Paula Saukko (2000). Between voice and discourse: quilting interviews on Anorexia. *Qualitative Inquiry*, 6, pp. 299–317.

7. See a discussion on the works of the practice of writing and the "spatial event" of the text in Angharad Saunders (2013). The spatial event of writing: John Galsworthy and the creation of Fraternity. *Cultural Geographies*, 20(3), pp. 285–298.

2 THE USES OF NOSTALGIA: RE-ENACTING SPACE AND TIME

1. To read other works on memory and space see Stephen Legg (2005). Contesting and surviving memory: space, nation, and nostalgia in *Les Lieux de Mémoire*. *Environment and Planning D: Society and Space*, 23, pp. 481–504; Maria N. Yelenevskaya and Larisa Fialkova (2002). When Time and space are no longer the same: stories about immigration. *Studia Mythologica Slavica V*, Vol. 5, pp. 207–230.

2. See also Claude Raffestin (2012). Space, territory, and territoriality. *Environment and Planning D: Society and Space*, 30, pp. 121–141; Deborah Youdell (2006) Subjectivation and performative politics- Butler thinking Althusser and Foucaul: intelligibility, agency and the raced-nationed-religioned subjects of education. *British Journal of Sociology of Education*, 27(4), pp. 511–528.

3. See also Lilian Chee (2012). The domestic residue: feminist mobility and space in Simrym Gill's art. *Gender, Place & Culture: A Journal of Feminist Geography*, 19(6), pp. 750–770; Carey-Ann Morrison (2010). Heterosexuality and Home: intimacies of space and spaces of touch. *Emotion, Space and Society*, xxx, pp. 1–9.

4. See also Lauren Berlant (2008). Thinking about Feeling Historical. *Emotion, Space and Society*, 1, pp. 4–9.

3 MOVING BODIES—HOW DO WE DO TIME AND SPACE

1. Most of these studies present unitary and essentialized notions of the international student therefore the ways to narrate their experiences and decisions made to study abroad follow the same pattern. Some of these discourses have been presented in several chapters of this book. As the field of internationalization of higher education is characterized by its managerial emphases most of the studies reinforce discourses on retention, attraction, and problems associated to the "cultural shock" to live outside of the home country.

2. See more discussions on atmosphere, affect, emotions, and space in Ben Anderson (2009). Affective Atmospheres. *Emotion,*

Space and Society, 2, pp. 77–81. On fear see Brian Massumi (1993). Everywhere you want to be, Introduction to Fear, in the *Politics of Every Fear*. Minneapolis: University of Minnesota Press, pp. 3–38; Joyce Davidson and Christine Milligan (2004). Embodying emotion sensing space: introducing emotional geographies. *Social & Cultural Geography*, 5(4), pp. 523–532.

3. See also Jennie Middleton (2009) "Stepping in time": walking, time, and space in the city. *Environment and Planning A*, 41, pp. 1943–1961, to understand the politics of experiential dimensions of time.

4 THE STRANGE BODY

1. Also see Anastasia Christou (2011). Narrating lives in (e)motion: embodiment, belongingness and displacement in diasporic spaces of home and return. *Emotion, Space and Society*, 4, pp. 249–257 for a discussion on a narrative turn on migration studies to explore on the embodied and emotional dimensions of migration and return migration. She explores on the embodied contexts of how belonging and exclusion shape mobilities. Also see Joyce Davidson and Christine Milligan (2004). Embodying emotion sensing space: introducing emotional geographies. *Social & Cultural Geography*, 5(4), pp. 523–532.

2. See Stephen Ball (2012). Performativity, commodification and commitment: an I-spy guide to the Neoliberal University. *British Journal of Education Studies*, 60(1), pp. 17–28.

3. See an interesting discussion on how time becomes "real" and how we come to know it and the effects of how time, real time is communicated. Tung-Hui Hu (2012). Real time/zero time. *Discourse*, 34(2–3), pp. 163–184.

4. More on the production of particular subjectivities, sexuality, and space in Judith Halberstam (2005). *In a Queer Time and Space. Transgender Bodies, Subcultural Lives*. New York and London: New York University Press; Eithne Luibheid (2002). *Entry Denied. Controlling Sexuality at the Border*. Minneapolis: University of Minnesota Press; Catherine J. Nash (2010). Trans geographies, embodiment, and experience. *Gender, Place & Culture. A Journal*

of Feminist Geography, 17(5), 579–595; Gulsum Baydar (2012). Sexualised productions of space. *Gender, Place & Culture: A Journal of Feminist Geography,* 19(6), pp. 699–706; Marlene Spanger (2013). Gender performances as spatial acts: (fe)male Thai migrant sex workers in Denmark. *Gender, Place & Culture: A Journal of Feminis Geography,* 20(1), pp. 37–52.

5 LANDSCAPES OF THE BODY: DESIRING SPACE OTHERWISE

1. See Caren Kaplan (1996). *Questions of Travel, Postmodern Discourses of Displacement.* Durahm and London: Duke University Press; Erin Manning (2007). *Politics of Touch. Sense, Movement, Sovereignty.* Minneapolis: University of Minnesota Press; Brian Massumi (2011). *Semblance and Event. Activist Philosophy and the Ocurrent Arts.* Cambridge, MA: MIT Press.
2. See Erin Manning (2009). The Elasticity of the Almost. In Erin Manning (Ed.) *Relationscapes. Movement, Art, Philosophy.* Cambridge, MA: MIT Press, pp. 29–42.
3. For a complete philosophical discussion on the distinction between space and place see Edward S. Casey (1997). *The Fate of Place. A Philosophical History.* Berkeley: University of California Press. Also see David Featherston and Joe Painter (eds.) (2013). *Spatial Politics. Essays for Doreen Massey.* Chichester, NJ: Wiley-Blackwell.
4. See also David Crouch (2003). Spacing, performing, and becoming: tangles in the mundane. *Environment and Planning A,* 35, pp. 1945–1960.
5. See Kalpana Rahita Seshadri (2008). When home is a camp. Global Sovereignty, Biopolitics and Internally Displaced Persons. *Social Text,* 94, 29(1), pp. 29–58.

6 WOMEN AND TRAVEL: TEMPORAL IMAGINARIES OF BECOMING

1. See also E. L. McCallum and Mikko Tuhkanen (2011). Introduction. Becoming Unbecoming. Untimely Mediations. In E. L. McCallum amd Mikko Tuhkanen (eds.) *Queer*

Times, Queer Becomings. New York: Suny Press, pp. 1–21; Tim Dean (2011). Bareback Time. In E. L. McCallum and Mikko Tuhkanen (eds.) *Queer Times, Queer Becomings.* New York: Suny Press, pp. 75–98.

2. For a discussion on how the state has produced particular campuses as national and local expressions of forces of Fordism and neoliberalism, see also Bernd Belina, Tino Petzold, Jürgen Schardt and Sebastian Schippe (2013). Neoliberalism and the Fordist University: a tale of two campuses in Frankfurt a. M., Germany. *Antipode,* 45(3), pp. 738–759.

3. She speaks from an administrative position, which is a very common activity performed by women academics when they are back to universities.

7 WOMEN AND THE POLITICS OF WRITING

* These ideas were presented at the XVIII ISA World Congress of Sociology, Yokohama, Japan 2014. The title of the paper was "Academic Writing as a Contesting Territory for Women."

1. In Chilean universities there is a strong pressure for academics to write in specific journals. Usually they have to belong to the ISI and SCOPUS databases. These have become the criteria for academic evaluations and a way to rank professors to obtain funding for research.

2. This is particularly relevant in the European scenario where the European Credit System ECTS, promotes a unified system of accreditation of credit points. These Bologna initiatives are to advance student mobility, to enhance the capacity of universities to compete internationally, and to promote the employability of graduates.

CONCLUSIONS DISSOLVING

1. NAFSA is a US nonprofit organization for professional in all areas of international education including English as a Second Language, international student advising, education abroad advising and administration, campus internationalization among others.

References

Abel, Carolyn (2002a). Family Adjustment to American Culture. *New Directions for Higher Education*, 117: 71–77.

Abel, Charles (2002b). Academic Success and the International Student: Research and Recommendations. *New Directions for Higher Education*, 117: 13–20.

Ahmed, S. (2000). *Strange Encounters. Embodied Others in Post-Coloniality.* London and New York: Routledge.

Ahmed, S. (2004). *The Cultural Politics of Emotions.* New York: Routledge.

Ahmed, S. (2006). *Queer Phenomenology. Orientations, Objects, Others.* Durham, NC and London: Duke University Press.

Ahmed, S. (2010). *The Promise of Happiness.* Durham, NC and London: Duke University Press.

Allon, F. (2000). Nostalgia Unbound: Illegibility and the Synthetic Excess of Place. *Continuum: Journal of Media & Cultural Studies*, 14 (3): 275–287.

Alarcon, N., C. Kaplan, and M. Moallen (1999). Introduction: Between Woman and Nation. In *Between Woman and Nation. Nationalisms, Transnational Feminisms, and the State.* Durham, NC and London: Duke University Press, pp. 1–16.

Alcoff, L. (1999). Becoming an Epistemologist. In E. Grosz (ed.), *Becomings. Exploration in Time, Memory, and Futures.* Ithaca, NY and London: Cornell University Press, pp. 55–75.

Altbach. P. G. (2001). Higher Education and the WTO: Globalization Run Amok [Electronic version]. *International Higher Education*, 23: 2–5. Retrieved May 20, 2003 from https://www.bc.edu/content/dam/files/research_sites/cihe/pdf/IHEpdfs/ihe23.pdf

Altbach, P. G. (2002). Knowledge and Education as International Commodities: The Collapse of the Common Good. [Electronic version]. *International Higher Education*, 28: 2–5. Retrieved May

20, 2003 from https://www.bc.edu/content/dam/files/research_sites/cihe/pdf/IHEpdfs/ihe28.pdf

Aronowitz, S. (2000). *The Knowledge Factory. Dismantling the Corporeate University and Creating True Higher Learning.* Boston: Bacon Press.

Arum, S. and J. van de Water (1992). The Need for a Definition of International Education in U.S. Universities. In Ch. B. Klasek, B. J. Garavilia, K. J. Kellerman, and B. B. Marx (eds.), *Bridges to the Future: Strategies for Internationalizing Higher Education.* Association of International Education Administrators. Carbondale, IL: Southern Illinois University at Carbondale, pp. 191–203.

Atia, N. and J. Davies (2010). Nostalgia and the Shapes of History. *Memory Studies* 3(3): 181–186.

Barry, A., T. Osborne, and N. Rose (1996). Introduction. In A. Barry, T. Osborne, and N. Rose (eds.), *Foucault and Political Reason: Liberalism, Neo-Liberalism, and Rationalities of Government.* Chicago: University of Chicago Press, pp. 1–17.

Bakhtin, M. (1981). *The Dialogic Imagination,* trans. Caryl Emerson and Michael Holquist. Austin: University of Texas Press.

Baydar, Gulsum. (2012). Sexualised Productions of Space. *Gender, Place & Culture: A Journal of Feminist Geography,* 19(6): 699–706.

Bordo, S. (1986). The Cartesian Masculinization of Thought. *Signs,* 11(3): 439–456.

Britzman, D. (1992). The Terrible Problem of Knowing Thyself: Toward a Poststructural Account of Teacher Identity. *Journal of Curriculum Theorizing,* 9(3): 23–46.

Britzman, D. (2000). "Question of Belief": Writing Poststructural Ethnography. In Wanda Pillow and Elizabeth St. Pierre (eds.), *Working the Ruins: Feminist Poststructural Theory and Methods in Education.* New York and London: Routledge, pp. 27–40.

Brown, K., C. Nash, and J. Heckert (2010). Queer Methods and Methodologies. An Introduction. In Kath Browne and Catherine J Nash (eds.), *Queer Methods and Methodologies. Intersecting Queer Theories and Social Science Research.* England: Ashgate, pp. 1–24.

Brunner, J. J., et al. (1993). *Paradigmas de Conocimiento y Práctica Social en Chile.* Chile: Flacso.

Butler, J. (1993). Bodies that Matter: on the Discursive Limits of "Sex": New York: Routledge.

Calhoun, C. (2003). The Class Consciousness of Frequent Travellers: Towards a Critique of Actually Existing Cosmopolitanism. In Daniele Archibugi (ed.), *Debating Cosmopolitics*. London: Bath Press, pp. 68–86.

Casey, E. (1999). The Time of the Glance: Toward Becoming Otherwise. In E. Grosz (ed.), *Becomings. Exploration in Time, Memory, and Futures*. Ithaca, NY and London: Cornell University Press, pp. 29–41

Clifford, J. (1988). *The Predicament of Culture. Twentieth-Century Ethnography, Literature, and Arts*. Cambridge: Harvard University Press.

Clifford J. (1989). Notes on Travel and Theory. Inscriptions, N.5 [Electronic version]. Retrieved July 7, 2003 from http://hum-www.ucsc.edu/Divweb/CultStudies/PUBS/Inscriptions/vol_5/v5_top.html.

Clifford, J. (1997). *Routes. Travel and Translation in the Late Twentieth Century*. Cambridge: Harvard University Press.

Clough, T. P. and J. Jean Halley (eds.) (2007). *The Affective Turn. Theorizing the Social*. Durham, NC and London: Duke University Press.

Cheah, P. (1999). Spectral Nationality: The Living-On [sur–vie] of the Postcolonial Nation in Neocolonial Globalization. In E. Grosz (ed.), *Becomings. Explorations of Time, Memory, and Futures*. Ithaca, NY and London: Cornell University Press, pp. 176–200.

Colebrook, C. (1996). A Grammar of Becoming. In Elizabeth Grosz (ed.), *Becomings. Explorations in Time, Memory, and Futures*. Ithaca, NY and London: Cornell University Press, pp. 117–140.

Cummins, W. (2001). Current Changes of International Education. Office of Educational Research and Improvement, Washington, DC. Retrieved May 5, 2003 from http//www.eriche.org.

Davis, B. (2000). Eclipsing the Constitutive Power of Discourse: The Writing of Janette Turner Hospital. In Wanda Pillow and Elizabeth St. Pierre (eds.), *Working the Ruins: Feminist Poststructural Theory and Methods in Education*. New York and London: Routledge, pp. 179–198.

Davies, J. L. (1992). Developing a Strategy for Internationalization in Universities: Towards a Conceptual Framework. In Ch. B. Klasek, B. J. Garavilia, K. J. Kellerman, and B. B. Marx (eds.), *Bridges to the Future: Strategies for Internationalizing Higher Education.* Association of International Education Administrators. Carbondale, IL: Southern Illinois University at Carbondale, pp. 177–190.

Davidson-Harden (2009). Neoliberalism, Knowledge Capitalism, and the Steered University: The Role of OECD and the Canadian Federal Government Discourse. In M. Peters, A. C. Besley, M. Olsen, S. Mauren, and S. Weber (eds), *Governmentality Studies in Education.* Rotterdam: Sense Publishers, pp. 271–302.

De Landa, M. (1999). Deleuze, Diagrams, and the Open-Ended Becoming of the World. In E. Grosz (ed.), *Becomings. Exploration in Time, Memory, and Futures.* Ithaca, NY and London: Cornell University Press, pp. 29–41.

Deleuze, G. and F. Guattari (1987). *A Thousand Plateaus. Capitalism and Schizophrenia.* Minneapolis and London: University of Minnesota Press.

Denzin, N. (2000) *Handbook of Qualitative Research.* Thousand Oaks: Sage.

Duggan, L. (2003). *The Twilight of Equality. Neoliberalism, Cultural Politics, and the Attack on Democracy.* Boston, MA: Beacon Press.

Fairclough, N. (2003). *Analysing Discourse: Textual Analysis for Social Research.* New York: Routledge.

Francis, A. (1993). *Facing the Future: The Internationalization of Postsecondary Institutions in British Columbia. Task Force Report.* Vancouver, Canada: Centre for International Education.

Foster, H. (1985). Recordings: art, spectacle, cultural politics. Port Townsend, Washington: Bay Press.

Game, A. (2001). Belonging: Experience in Sacred Time and Space. In Jon May and Nigel Thrift (eds.), *TimeSpace. Geographies of Temporality.* London and New York: Routledge, pp. 226–239.

Gee, J. P. (1999). *An Introduction to Discourse Analysis: Theory and Method.* New York and London: Routledge.

Gilroy, P. (1991). It Ain't Where You're from, It's Where You're at... The Dialectics of Diasporic Identification. *Third Text* 13: 3–16.

Grosz, E. (1994). A Thousand Tiny Sexes: Feminism and Rhizomatics. In C. V. Boundas and D. Olkowski (eds.), *Gilles Deleuze and the theater of philosophy*. New York: Routledge, pp. 187–210.

Grosz, E. (1995). *Space, Time, and Perversion. Essays on the Politics of Bodies*. New York and London: Routledge.

Grosz, E. (ed.) (1999). *Becomings. Explorations in Time, Memory, and Futures*. Ithaca, NY and London: Cornell University Press.

Grosz, E. (2004). *The Nick of Time. Politics, Evolution, and the Untimely*. Durham, NC and London: Duke University Press.

Grosz, E. (2005). *Time Travels. Feminism, Nature, Power*. Durham, NC and London: Duke University Press.

Grossberg, L. (2000). History and Imagination and the Politics of Belonging: Between the Death and the Fear of History. In Paul Gilroy, Lawrence Grossberg, and Angela Mc Robins (eds.), *Without Guarantees in Honour of Stuart Hall*. New York: Verso, pp. 148–164.

Gudykunst, W. (1998). *Bridging Differences. Effective Intergroup Communication*. Thousand Oaks: Sage.

Gudykunst, W. (2003). *Culture and Interpersonal Communication*. Thousand Oaks: Sage.

Hall, S. (1996). Who Needs "Identity?." In S. Hall and P. du Gay (eds.), *Questions of Cultural Identity*. London: Sage, pp. 1–17.

Haraway, Donna, (1988). Situated Knowledges: The Science Question in Feminism and the Privilege of Partial Perspective. *Feminist Studies*, 14(3): 575–599.

Hetherington, K. (2001). Moderns as Ancients. Time, Space, and the Discourse of Improvement. In J. May and N. Thrift (eds.), *TimeSpace. Geographies of Temporality*. London and New York: Routledge, pp. 49–72.

Hodder, I. (2000). The Interpretation of Documents and Material Culture. In N. Denzin and Y. Lincoln (eds.), *Handbook of Qualitative Research*. Thousand Oaks: Sage.

Hohne, Th. and B. Schrech (2009). Modularized Knowledge. In M. Peters, A. C. Besley, M. Olsen, S. Mauren, and S. Weber (eds.), *Governmentality Studies in Education*. Rotterdam: Sense Publishers, pp. 499–508.

Institute of International Education (2002). Open doors report on international education exchange. Retrived from http://www.iie. org/opendoors.

Iuspa, F. (2014). Assessing a Historically Hispanic Serving Institution Internationalization Process. *Sage Open*, 4(3): 1–14.

Jameson, F. (1981). *The Political Unconscious: Narrative as a Socially Symbolic Act.* Ithaca: Cornell University Press.

Johnson, N. (2001). From Time Inmemorial: narratives of nationhood and the making of national space. In J. May and N. Thrift (eds.), *TimeSpace. Geographies of Temporality.* London and New York: Routledge, pp. 89–105.

Keith, M. and S. Pile (1993). *Place and the Politics of Identity.* London: Routledge.

Kellner, D. (1992). Popular Culture and the Construction of Postmodern Identities. In S. Lash and J. Friedman (eds.), *Modernity & Identity.* Oxford: Blackwell, pp. 141–177.

Kirp, D. L. (2003). *Shakespeare, Einstein, and the Bottom Line: The Marketing of Higher Education.* Cambridge, MA: Harvard University Press.

Klasek, Ch. B., B. J. Garavilia, K. J. Kellerman, and B. B. Marx (1992). *Bridges to the Future: Strategies for Internationalizing Higher Education.* Association of International Education Administrators. Carbondale, IL: Southern Illinois University at Carbondale.

Knight, J. and H. de Wit (1995). Strategies for Internationalization of Higher Education: Historical and Conceptual Perspectives. In H. de Wit (ed.), *Strategies for Internationalization of Higher Education: A Comparative Study of Australia, Canada, Europe and the United States.* Amsterdam: European Association for International Education, pp. 5–32.

Kristeva, J. (1980). *Desire in Language: A Semiotic Approach to Literature and Art.* New York: Columbia University Press.

Kuhlman, A. (1992). Foreign Students and Scholars. In Klasek, Ch. B., B. J. Garavilia, K. J. Kellerman, and B. B. Marx (eds.), *Bridges to the Future: Strategies for Internationalizing Higher Education.* Association of International Education Administrators. Carbondale, IL: Southern Illinois University at Carbondale, pp. 22–38.

Lacina, J. (2002). Preparing International Students for a Successful Social Experience in Higher Education. *New Directions for Higher Education*, 117: 21–27.

Lather, P. (2007). *Getting Lost. Feminist Efforts toward a Double(d) Science*. Albany: State University of New York Press.

Lyotard, J. F. (1984). *The Postmodern Condition: A Report on Knowledge*. Minneapolis: University of Minnesota Press

Lee Carlson, David (2009). Producing Entrepreneurial Subjects: Neoliberal Rationalities and Portfolio Assessment. In M. Peters, A. C. Besley, M. Olsen, S. Mauren, and S. Weber (eds.), *Governmentality Studies in Education*. Rotterdam: Sense Publishers, pp. 257–270.

Lowenthal, D. (1985). Relieving the Past: Dreams and Nightmares. In David Lowenthal (ed.), *The Past Is a Foreign Country*. Cambridge: Cambridge University Press, pp. 3–34.

Lulat, Y. and P. G. Altbach (1985). International Students in Comparative Perspective. Toward a Political Economy of International Study. In J. Smart (ed.) *Higher Education: Handbook of Theory and Research*. New York: Agathon Press, pp. 439–494.

Lyotard, J.-F. (1979). *The Postmodern Condition: A Report on Knowledge*. Minneapolis: University of Minnesota Press.

Manning, E. (2003). *Ephimeral Territories. Representing Nation, Home, and Identity in Canada*. Minneapolis and London: University of Minnesota Press.

Manning, E. (2009). *Relationscapes. Movement, Art, Philosophy*. Cambridge: MIT Press.

Marin N. (1996). *Intercultural Challenges for Foreign Students into the Stressful Journey of Graduate School*. Paper presented at the Annual Meeting of the Speech Communication Association, 82nd., San Diego, CA.

Marginson, S., and M. Considine (2000). *The Enterprise University: Power, Governance, and Reinvention in Australia*. New York: Cambridge University Press.

Massey, D. (1993). Politics and Space/Time. In Michael Keith and Steve Pile (eds.), *Place and the Politics of Identity*. London and New York: Routledge, pp. 141–161.

Massey, D. (1994). *Space, Place, and Gender*. Minneapolis: University of Minnesota Press.

Massey, D. (2005). *For space.* London: Sage.

Massumi, B. (2002). *Parables for the Virtual: Movement, Affect, Sensation.* Durham, NC and London: Duke University Press.

Matus, C. (2006). Interrupting Narratives of Displacement: International Students in the U.S. *Perspectives on Education* (Special Issue: Internationalisation of Higher Education: Global Challenges, Regional Impacts, and National Responses), 24(4): 81–91.

Matus, C. and S. Talburt (2009). Spatial Imaginaries: Universities, Internationalization, and Feminist Geographies. *Discourse: Studies in the Cultural Politics of Education*, 31(1): 515–527.

McDowell, L. (1999). *Gender, Identity and Place. Understanding Feminist Geographies.* Minneapolis: University of Minnesota Press.

McHoul, A. and W. Grace (1997). *A Foucault Primer: Power and the Subject.* New York: New York University Pres.

McWilliam, E. (2000). Laughin within Reason: On Pleasure, Women, and Academic Performance. In Elizabeth St. Pierre and Wanda Pillow (eds.), *Working the Ruins. Feminist Poststructural Theory and Methods in Education.* NewYork: Routledge, pp. 164–178.

Mills, S. (1997). *Discourse.* London and New York: Routledge.

Minnich, K. E. (2005). *Transforming Knowledge.* Philadelphia: Temple University Press.

Miyoshi, M. (2000). Ivory Tower in Escrow. *Boundary 2*, 27(1): 7–50.

Moya, P. and M. R. Hames-Garcia (2000). *Reclaiming Identity. Realist Theory and the Predicament of Postmodernism.* Berkeley, California: University of California Press.

National Association of International Educators (NAFSA) (2003). "Securing America's Future: Global Education for a Global Age," downloaded at http://www.nafsa.org/uploadedFiles/ NAFSA_Home/Resource_Library_Assets/Public_Policy/securing_america_s_future.pdf.

NAFSA (2005). "Measuring and Assessing Internationalization" by Madeleine Green, downloaded at, http://www.nafsa.org/ uploadedFiles/NAFSA_Home/Resource_Library_Assets/ Publications_Library/Measuring%20and%20Assessing%20 Internationalization.pdf.

NAFSA (2007). "Internaitonalizing the Campus. Profiles of Success at Colleges + Universities," downloaded at http://www.nafsa.org/_/file/_/itc2007.pdf.

Nelson, C. and S. Watt (1999). The Corporate University. In: C. Nelson and S. Watt (eds.), *Academic Keywords: A Devil's Dictionary for Higher Education*. New York: Routledge, pp. 84–98.

Olkowski, D. (1999). Flows of Desire and the Body-Becoming. In E. Grosz (ed.), *Becomings. Exploration in Time, Memory, and Futures*. Ithaca, NY and London: Cornell University Press, pp. 98–116.

Patrick, K. (1997). *Internationalising the University: Implications for Teachning and Learning at RMIT Royal Melbourne Institute of Technology*. Retrieved May 2000 from http://teaching.rmit.edu.au/resources/index.html.

Peters, M. (1992). Performance and Accountability in "Post-Industrial Society": the Crisis of British Universities. *Studies in Higher Education* 17: 123–139.

Peters, M. (2002). The University in the Knowledge Economy. In S. Cooper, J. Hinkson, and G. Sharp (eds.), *Scholars and Entrepreneurs: The Universities in Crisis*. North Carlton, Australia: Arena, pp. 137–151.

Peters, M., A. C. Besley, M. Olsen, S. Mauren, and S. Weber (eds.) (2009).*Governmentality Studies in Education*. Rotterdam: Sense Publishers.

Petrunic, A.-M. (2005). No Man's Land: The Intersection of Balkan Space and Identity. *History of Intellectual Culture*, 5(1): 1–10.

Rajchman, J. (1999). Diagram and Diagnosis. In E. Grosz, *Becomings. Exploration in Time, Memory, and Futures*. Ithaca, NY and London: Cornell University Press, pp. 42–54.

Radstone, S. (2007). *The Sexual Politics of Time. Confession, nostalgia, memory*. London and New York: Routledge.

Rahman, T. and L. Kopp (1992). Administration of International Education. In Ch. B. Klasek, B. J. Garavilia, K. J. Kellerman, and B. B. Marx (eds.), *Bridges to the Future: Strategies for Internationalizing Higher Education*. Association of International Education Administrators. Carbondale, IL: Southern Illinois University at Carbondale, pp. 1–21.

Rasmussen, M. L. (2004). "That's So Gay!": A Study of the Deployment of Signifiers of Sexual and Gender Identity in Secondary School Settings in Australia and the United States. *Social Semiotics*, 14(3): 289–308.

Readings, B. (1996). *The University in Ruins*. Cambridge, MA: Harvard University Press.

Richardson, L (2000). Skirting a Pleated Text: De-Discipline an Academic Life. In Elizabeth St. Pierre and Wanda Pillow (eds.), *Working the Ruins. Feminist Poststructural Theory and Methods in Education*. New York: Routledge, pp. 153–163.

Rizvi, F. (2000). International Education and the Global Production of Global Imagination. In N. Burbules and C. A. Torres (eds.), *Globalization and Education. Critical Perspectives*. New York: Routledge, pp.205–225.

Rizvi, F., R. Lingard, S. Taylor, and M. Henry (2001). *Globalization, the OECD and Educational Policy*. Oxford: Pergamon.

Rodriguez, A.P. (2000). Adjusting the multicultural lens. *Race, Gender & Class*, 7(3), 150–177.

Sadiki, L. (2001). *Internationalising the Curriculum in the 21st Century*. Centre for Educational Development and Academic Methods (CEDAM), Australian National University. Retrieved May, 2002 from http://anu.edu.au/CEDAM/internationalc.html.

Sakurako, M. (2000). Addressing the Mental Health Concerns of International Students. *Journal of Counseling & Development*, 78(2): 137–144.

Sarup, M. (1996). *Identity, Culture and the Postmodern World*. Athens, GA: University of Georgia Press.

Scott, J. (1991). The Evidence of Experience. *Critical Inquiry*, 17: 773–797.

Sidhu, R. (2006). *Universities and Globalization: To Market, to Market*. Mahwah, NJ: Lawrence Erlbaum.

Sidhu, R. (2007). GATS and the New Developmentalism: Governing Transnational Eudcation. *Comparative Education Review*, 51 (2): 203–227.

Sidhu, R. and G. D'Alba (2012). International Education and (Dis) embodied Cosmopolitanisms. *Educational Philosophy and Theory*, 44(4): 413–431.

Sharma, S. (2014). *In the Meantime. Temporality and Cultural Politics*. Durham, NC and London: Duke University Press.

Slaughter, Sh. and L.Leslie (1997). *Academic Capitalism: Politics, Policies, and the Entrepreneurial University.* Baltimore, MD: Johns Hopkins University Press.

Slaughter, Sh. and G. Rhoades (2004). *Academic Capitalism and the New Economy: Markets, State, and Higher Education.* Baltimore, MD: Johns Hopkins University Press.

Smith, N. and C. Katz (1993). Grounding Metaphor: Towards a Spatialized Politics. In M. Keith and S. Pile (eds.), *Place and the Politics of Identity.* London and New York: Routledge, pp. 67–83.

St. Pierre, E. (1997). Nomadic Inquiry in the Smooth Spaces of the Field: A Preface. *International Journal of Qualitative Studies in Education,* 10(3): 365–383.

Stewart, K. (1988). Nostalgia—a Polemic. *Cultural Anthropology,* 3: 227–241.

Stewart, K. (1996). *A Space on the Side of the Road. Cultural Poetics in an "Other" America.* Princeton, NJ: Princeton University Press.

Stewart, K. (2007). *Ordinary Affects.* Durham: Duke University Press.

Trice, Andrea. (2000). *Faculty Perceptions of Graduate International Students: the Benefits and Challenges.* Paper Presented at the Annual Meeting of the Association for the Study of Higher Education, Richmond VA.

Tsolidis, G. (2008). The (Im)possibility of Poststructuralist Ethnography-Researching Identities in Borrowed Spaces. *Ethnography and Education,* 3(3): 271–281.

Valis, N. (2000). Nostalgia and Exile. *Journal of Spanish Cultural Studies,* 1(2): 117–133.

Weedon, Chris (1999). *Feminism, Theory, and the Politics of Difference.* Oxford: Blackwell.

Weems, Lisa (2010). From "Home" to "Camp:" Theorizing the Space of Safety. *Studies in Philosophy of Education* 29(6): 557–568.

Weinbaum, A. E. (2007). Nation. In B. Burgett and G. Hendler (eds.), *Keywords for American Cultural Studies.* New York and London: New York University Press, pp. 164–170.

Wilson, R. and W. Dissanayake (1996). Introduction: Tracking the Global/Local. In *Global/Local: Cultural Production and the Transnational Imaginary.* Durham, NC: Duke University Press, pp. 1–18.

INDEX

Literature, academic discipline of,
157–60, 169
Lulat, Y., 96, 99
Lyotard, J. F., 132, 142, 143–4, 158–9

Manning, Erin, 28, 36, 113
on historiography, 118
on home, 54
on national identity, 117
on national vocabulary and
semantics, 57, 59
and qualified and unqualified bodies,
176
Massey, Doreen, 4, 23–4, 28, 31, 36
on definitions of time and space, 2–3,
44, 136–7
on identity, 52, 97, 83, 116, 120, 126
on imagination of space, 24, 50, 52,
96, 107, 111, 121
on meeting places, 125–6
on nostalgia, 44, 52
on place, 46, 52, 83, 111–12, 116,
120, 121, 123, 125–6
on space and knowledge production,
105
on space and social construction, 97,
112, 123
Massumi, Brian, 2, 4, 36, 87, 108, 167
on divided time, 131
on imagination of space, 111
on movement, 25, 27, 124, 113–14,
143
on paths, 124, 177
and politics of space, 167, 168
on positionality, 109–10, 113
on position-gridded space, 137
on time, 105
McDowell, 116, 122–3
meaning, 16, 53, 56, 65, 79, 82
of being an academic, 6–8
cultural, 1, 8
habitual/taken-for-granted, 1, 19–20
and methodology, 23, 25–8, 30,
32–7, 39–41
movement of meaning, 18
and writing, 39–40, 163–4

Merleau-Ponty, Maurice, 89
methodology
and bodies in motion, 16–18, 27, 30,
37–41
discourse analysis, 16
and dominant ideas of space and
time, 23, 25, 27, 29–30, 32–3,
36–8
and feminist theory, 18
and gender theory, 18
interviews, 16, 18–19, 20, 26–35, 37,
39–40
and looking back, 34–5
narratives, 33–5
and query theory, 18
See also narratives
migration, 9, 18, 51, 94, 96, 110,
191n1
Minnich, K. E., 152
modernism, 8, 51–2, 91, 100, 154, 179
movement
and gender, 57–60, 129–49
imaginary and material, 183
international students' experiences of,
63–83
and nostalgia, 45, 48, 54, 56–60
and paths, 129, 131–2, 143
and place, 108, 110–16, 118, 123–4,
126
transformative attribute of, 114
Moya, P., 78–9
multiplicity, 3, 9, 21, 52, 98, 183–4

NAFSA. *See* American Council of
Education and the Association of
International Educators (NAFSA)
narratives
Ann (Turkey), 65–6, 71–2
Javiera (Colombia), 66, 71, 75–82
Kenyan male narrative of space, 56–9
Peter (Kenya), 66–7, 73–4
Sarah (Japan), 31, 67–8, 72
Turkish woman narrative of space,
53–6
nation and nation-states, 18, 121, 124
and belonging, 40